Communist Agriculture

Farming in the Far East and Cuba

The role of agriculture and the peasantry is a central feature of Marxist-Leninist theory and a crucial problem of practice in the basically agrarian countries where communist regimes have become established. Yet few people have more than a superficial knowledge of the agrarian systems in these countries, or of the changes many of them are undergoing. This volume is an important contribution to our understanding of these changes which are described and analysed as of early 1988.

Focusing on Asian countries with communist regimes and on Cuba, the book describes their experience. It traces the adaptation necessary to the Marxist-Leninist ideology originally adopted in these countries in order to meet prevailing conditions of agricultural production and outlines a process of change which is continuing today. The contributors, all experts in their special fields, discuss how the Soviet experience has influenced and sometimes hindered development, and look in detail at agricultural development and agrarian policies in China, Mongolia, Vietnam and Cuba.

Together with its companion volume, *Communist Agriculture: Farming in the Soviet Union and Eastern Europe*, the book will be of value not only to students and teachers of socialist systems, political science, and geography, but to those studying comparative agricultural and developmental economics.

The Editor
Karl-Eugen Wädekin was until recently Professor at the University of Giessen, West Germany. An expert on socialist agriculture, he is the author of *The Private Sector in Soviet Agriculture* (1973) and *Agrarian Policies in Communist Europe* (1982) as well as four more books in German on related subjects.

Communist Agriculture

Farming in the Far East and Cuba

Edited by Karl-Eugen Wädekin

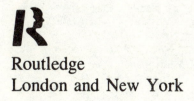

Routledge
London and New York

First published 1990 by Routledge
11 New Fetter Lane, London EC4P 4EE

Simultaneously published in the USA and Canada
by Routledge
a division of Routledge, Chapman and Hall, Inc.
29 West 35th Street, New York, NY 10001

© 1990 Karl-Eugen Wädekin

Phototypeset in 10pt Times by
Mews Photosetting, Beckenham, Kent
Printed in Great Britain by
Billing & Sons Ltd, Worcester

British Library Cataloguing in Publication Data

Communist agriculture: farming in the Far East and
    Cuba.
    1. Communist countries. Agricultural industries.
    Development
    I. Wädekin, Karl-Eugen
    338.1′09171′7

    ISBN 0-415-04205-4

Library of Congress-Cataloging-in-Publication Data

Communist agriculture: farming in the Far East and Cuba / edited by
    Karl-Eugen Wädekin.
         p. cm.
    Selected papers presented at the 8th International Conference on
Soviet and East European Agricultural Affairs, held in Berkeley Aug.
10–11, 1987.
    Includes index.
    ISBN 0-415-04205-4
    1. Communism and agriculture – Case studies – Congresses.
2. Agriculture and state – East Asia – Case studies – Congresses.
3. Agriculture and state – Cuba – Congresses. I. Wädekin, Karl-
Eugen. II. International Conference on Soviet and East European
Agricultural Affairs (8th : 1987 : Berkeley, Calif.)
HX550.A37C65   1990
630′.9171′7–dc20   89-10445
                                                        CIP

Contents

Tables

Preface

When the programme for the Eighth International Conference on Soviet and East European Agricultural Affairs, held at Berkeley, California, on 8–10 August, 1987, was conceived in 1986 and early in 1987, the organizers decided that in a collection of papers on present agricultural developments in the 'socialist world system', its non-European members should not be ignored. Three of these countries (Mongolia, Cuba and Vietnam) are also members of the Council of Mutual Economic Assistance (CMEA) under Soviet leadership, the other two (People's Republic of China and North Korea, officially called the Democratic People's Republic of Korea) are under regimes, which style themselves, and are generally considered to be, Marxist-Leninist. So a session of the conference was specially devoted to those countries.

Unfortunately, neither a paper, nor the discussions at Berkeley could be devoted to North Korea because the organizers did not know of any specialist on North Korean agriculture. Soviet and East European literature of recent years equally provides no, or very little, information on the subject. North Korean information policy as well as the language barrier seem to be the main reasons for this state of affairs.

The flow of information from China, Cuba and Mongolia is better. One of the most renowned Western specialists on Chinese agriculture, who is able to draw from the ever-growing literature and sources in Chinese, has contributed a paper. On Cuba and Mongolia, a certain amount of descriptions and analyses of the overall economy is available, but relatively little attention has been paid to agriculture. The language problem for Mongolia is not as severe as it might seem, as numerous Mongolian publications in Russian and other languages and also Soviet literature supply a considerable bulk of information on its agriculture. Concerning Vietnam, the organizers and the editor are happy to have won the co-operation of an author who knows not only the language but also has spent in total more than two years in Vietnam doing socio-economic research and then consulting for Western firms.

Not only Western specialized observers of Eastern Europe and the

Soviet Union, but also many communist leaders in those countries are little acquainted with the problems of peasant economies, where peasants live and produce not only under communist rule but also within agrarian systems very different from those of Europe or North America and where the communist regimes are confronted with the necessity of reform but do not want to overthrow the overall system.

The essays on the agriculture and agrarian policies of the four non-European countries as assembled in the present volume are meant mainly to serve a two-fold purpose: to present knowledge on what is less-known in the general public as well as among specialists on agriculture in communist and also in non-communist countries and to help drawing into mutual co-operation the observers and researchers of the European and the non-European socialist countries and also those of world-wide comparative agrarian policy.

K-E. Wädekin

Chapter one

Agrarian policies in China, Vietnam, Mongolia and Cuba[1]

Karl-Eugen Wädekin

The Soviet model and the 'reconsideration of ingrained notions'
The great challenge – Chinese agrarian policy
Vietnam – the less-known but important case
Similarities and diversity among the four countries
Communist agrarian reform under different conditions

The Soviet model and the 'reconsideration of ingrained notions'

Lenin had aimed at the proletarian revolution in predominantly agrarian Russia and therefore paid great attention to the role of the peasants in this revolution and the subsequent 'building of socialism'. The incorporation of the peasant question in the theory and practice forms one of the distinctive marks of Marxism-Leninism as different from original Marxism. The role of agriculture and the peasants has become a central issue of Marxist-Leninist theory and a crucial problem of practice in the basically agrarian countries where Communist regimes were being established. After the October Revolution the question of how to 'build socialism' against a recalcitrant peasantry, forming the great majority of a population under the 'dictatorship of the proletariat', exerted by a small communist elite, loomed large during the first decade of communist power in Russia and in what, by 1922, had become the Union of the Socialist Soviet Republics (USSR). Stalin's 'solution' to the problem was coercive collectivization combined with forceful industrialization and an extreme variant of dictatorship. Among those communist parties, which came to power in other countries, it was seen as a 'model', but proved counter-productive not only in Europe, but even more so in the less developed countries outside Europe.

Orthodox Marxists-Leninists are hard put to understand what is required and going on in China and Vietnam. Their difficulty is enhanced by the urge to reconcile the problems and necessary measures with Marxism-Leninism and their notion that this ideology is the best guide

1

for developing agrarian countries. Thus, two Soviet authors, whose book mixes valuable and sometimes even critical information with staunch Marxism-Leninism, had the following to say:

> The experience of Vietnam is one more confirmation of the truly international character of Lenin's co-operative plan, which represents the scientifically founded programme for the transition of the peasant masses on their way to socialism in countries with an undeveloped economy, one of which is Vietnam, as well as in countries with one or the other level of the development of capitalism on the countryside. . . . Lenin's ideas on the co-operativization of the peasantry and the rich experience of the USSR, of other socialist countries are being widely and in a creative way implemented in the Socialist Republic of Vietnam. (Isaev and Pivovarov, 1987: 199)

One wonders whether these authors were aware that it implied an indirect derogation of the transfer of the Soviet model, when they reported on the Sixth Congress of the Vietnamese CP of December, 1986 and its self-criticism of past mistakes – such as 'jumping over development stages', 'not making agriculture the foremost front of economic development', 'trends of unjustified enlargement of co-operatives' – and a few pages on quoted from a Soviet brochure of 1960: 'In the course of the agrarian transformation in the North the Vietnamese leaders widely used the Soviet experience in this question' (Isaev and Pivovarov, 1987: 72 and 77) In fact they also revealed a surprising lack of knowledge, when they wrote: 'An essential specialty of the production co-operation was the fact that it began and developed under preservation of the peasant property of land' (Isaev and Pivovarov, 1987: 199). Not only did the Vietnamese nationalize the land in 1980, but non-nationalization would not have been a special feature there, as in the whole of Eastern Europe land formally was not, or rather late and indirectly (in Romania and Albania), nationalized.

Another Soviet author, G.I. Shmelev, spelt out more clearly that the Soviet approach and model is not really applicable in countries like Vietnam and China. In his own country he has for years been speaking out in favour of private plots in combination with 'family link' contract production and seems to imply that rethinking is required, when he writes:

> It would be wrong to start from an evaluation of the course of events [in Vietnamese agriculture] on the basis of proclaimed principles. There is no doubt that in countries where a peasant population predominates in the period of unfinished construction of the fundaments of socialism and of insufficient development of the production forces and relationships, one cannot strictly and everywhere adhere

to agrarian policy principles and yet avoid certain economic and social costs at times of sharp changes of the organizational and economic structure. . . .

The introduction of family contracting [Shmelev uses the Russian term 'semeinyi podriad'] in Vietnam and China as well as some other ongoing new processes in the economic life of those countries demand the reconsideration of ingrained notions according to which the extension of experience among socialist countries must emanate exclusively from countries with a developed economy, which have gone a longer way of socialist construction [apparently, the USSR], towards countries with an underdeveloped economy, which have no rich historical experience of political and economic transformation of the society. (Schmelev, 1987a: 80, 81)

The great challenge – Chinese agrarian policy

After an initial peasant-orientated land reform period, Mao Zedong during 1953–7 proceeded along the lines of Soviet-type socialization of agriculture. By 1958, however, he obviously decided to overtake Moscow on the way to 'full communism' and started organizing a new form of giant rural enterprises, the People's Communes. The importance of these events and their subsequent course is obvious, not only because the Chinese peasantry is the most numerous in the world, but also because they were accompanied by the political rift between the USSR and China, without being its primary cause. The peripeties of the Chinese agrarian policies and their most recent period are well known, many books and articles in the main Western languages are available. C. Aubert's contribution on China to this volume (chapter 2) does not reiterate the story and instead dwells on the surplus of agricultural workers and the question of how to provide non-agricultural employment for them. In the longer run this may turn out to be China's most burning social and economic problem. The essay is a pioneering study indeed, but presupposes some knowledge of the development and present state of China's agriculture. Therefore, a very succinct general account is given below.

The People's Communes, which replaced the collective farms during the 'Great Leap Forward' campaign of 1958–9, were huge units of about 4,000 hectares on the average, and giant by numbers of workers, comprising roughly 5,000 peasant households. Their function was not only agricultural production, but also local government, creation of small- and mid-sized industries in the rural areas and mobilization of labour for great regional and supraregional construction works such as dams, roads, etc., as well as for territorial defence. As to agricultural production, the main level of organization within the Commune was that of the brigade of 100–150 hectares with the so-called team as its sub-unit.

Private plot and other private side-line production was severely restricted, private food markets driven into illegality. All this was done under strict discipline and low remuneration of work and in a headlong rush with little attention paid to economic considerations. It led to economic and social disaster, millions of people starved to death. After a short period of relaxation, 1961–3, when Mao was practically eliminated from power, he was able to resume his policy in most parts of the country (with some regional differences) during the turmoil period of the 'Cultural Revolution'. Again, hunger and destitution were widespread, certain regions experienced endemic crises of subsistence. The People's Communes survived as socio-political units yet were reduced in size, which by the early 1960s was roughly 2,000 hectares on average, while within them the teams (of about thirty families) had become the locus of basic production.

It was only after Mao's death (in 1976) and a few years of in-fighting among his successors that a fundamentally new course of agrarian, and general domestic, policy was embarked upon. Deng Xiaoping gradually re-emerged as the most powerful Chinese leader, and his policy led to the dismantling of the People's Communes during 1979–81 and their virtual abolition by 1982 (formalized in 1984). The 'responsibility system' became the cornerstone of agricultural organization, first in small teams, then almost exclusively with the peasant families as basic units. At present, they enjoy rather firm land usage rights of up to thirty or fifty years, while the property of all land remains with 'the people', that is, the State. One may speak of a form of long-term tenancy and, together with what in practice amounts to sub-tenancy, full possibility of non-agricultural activities within and outside the farm, free market access, etc. The term 'property rights' for individual peasants seems justified.

The growth of food and other agricultural output in China during the past decade (see Table 1.1), most of all during 1978–84, less so in more recent years, has been impressive, to say the least. Among its causes the reorganization of farming certainly represents a major, probably the main factor, but the impact of considerable rises in State procurement and free market prices for the producer was not negligible either. In addition, access to free markets, also beyond provincial borders, in parallel with decreasing obligatory procurement demands within a generally liberalized economy played a great role.

Vietnam – the less-known but important case

Few observers have noticed that at about the same time when the Chinese communists reinstated the peasant family as the basic unit of production, the Vietnamese leaders also returned to family production. And in the conquered southern part of Vietnam, which comprises 55 per cent of the country's total paddy land and yet more of its rice output, they have not yet, after such attempts, insisted on complete collectivization. However, they have not fully renounced collective farms, as the Chinese did, but rather made them an overhead organization for State procurements and input supplies. Although their attitude towards private plot production and the marketing of its output has become more tolerant, their agrarian and overall economic policy seems far from the Chinese degree of liberalization.

The chronological parallelism is very striking in view of the fact that in their ideology and foreign policy the two countries remain bitter adversaries, which makes it very unlikely that one followed the example of the other. The parallel is less striking, if one takes into account that in their natural and demographic endowment they show remarkable similarities, although Vietnam is even more typically characterized by intensive wet-rice (paddy) cultivation under a tropical climate than is China as a whole. Quite obviously it is the similar constraints and possibilities which forced the Vietnamese leaders to adopt a policy partly similar to that of China and running counter to their earlier intentions – apparently with Moscow's encouragement.

Adam Fforde in his contribution to the present volume has not only given an analysis of the recent developments in Vietnamese agriculture and agrarian policy, but in addition has broken fresh ground by presenting profound ideas on the difference of approach that is required for understanding the processes forming agricultural production and rural socio-economic life in Asian countries with traditions based on centuries of labour- and land-intensive wet-rice cultivation. As he concentrates mainly on this in-depth analysis and on the northern part of Vietnam with its collectivized agriculture, a few additional pieces of factual information are given below. This seems appropriate also because due to more than thirty years of a state of war in Vietnam and to seclusion from the outside world, little more than superficial information on the socio-economic conditions and development of its communist part has been available in the West. (As to Vietnam's natural endowment, the reader is referred to the Table 1.1).

It deserves emphasis that with 61.65 million inhabitants (end of 1986) Vietnam among the member countries of the CMEA (Council of Mutual Economic Assistance or Comecon; China is not a member) is second in population numbers only to the Soviet Union. Not only in foreign affairs it seems to aspire to a kind of South-east Asian 'Brezhnev doctrine' of guarding the political achievements of the socialist camp, but also in agrarian policy to a certain model function, as is implied in the following sentences from the Vietnamese daily *The People* (16 December 1986):

> The experience of the socialist transformation of the Vietnamese village with all its strong and a few weak sides has quite some

Table 1.1 Some basic data and indicators on the food economies of China, Vietnam, Mongolia and Cuba

	China[a]	Vietnam	Mongolia	Cuba
Population 1985, mill. annual average (China: end year)	1,045	59.9	1.9	10.1
1985 population index (1976 = 100)	116.7	121.8	126.9	106.6
1984–6 average index of agricultural gross production (1975–7 = 100)[b]	158.0	152.7	130.2	118.9
of which: crop production[b]	149.8	151.3	180.9	112.2
animal production[b]	208.8	152.8	113.7	130.8
Percentage of animal in overall agr. production, 1986	22.6[c]	24.2	67.2	34.9
Arable and permanent crop land as percentage of total land area	11	21	1	29
Arable and permanent crop land, mill. ha	100.7[d]	6.8	1.35	3.3
of which irrigated (%)	44	26	3	27
Permanent pasture, mill. ha	285.7	0.3	123.2	2.7
'Land units'[e] (a) mill. ha	157.8	6.8	26.0	3.8
(b) per head of total population, ha	0.15	0.11	13.3	0.37
'Livestock units'[f] per head of total population	0.17	0.13	3.17	0.64
Share of agricultural in total economically active population (FAO definition) in 1975 (%)	76.3	72.0	43.8	26.7
in 1986 (%)	70.3	63.4	34.0	21.0
Agricultural active population per 100 ha 'land units'[e]	280	273	1.2	23
Index 1984–6 of grain output (1974–76 = 100)	145[g]	143[g]	201	118
Grain output (kg) per head of total population, 1984–6 average	333[g]	262[g]	414	63
Grain yield, tonnes/hectare, 1984–6 average	3.6[h]	2.8[h]	1.2	2.5
Share of rice in grain sown area in 1986 (%)	37	84	–	63
Grain import/export balance per head of the population, kilograms per year, average 1984–6	6	8	1–2[i]	211[i]
Shares in agricultural land, 1986				
state farms and enterprises (%)	approx. 5	> 9[k]	11.4	84.7 (1985)
collective farms (excl. private plots) (%)	approx. 95	61.4	88.6	15.3 (1985)
rest (basically in private use) (%)		< 30[k]	10.0	0[j]

Notes:

(a) Most of the data for China are from FAO statistics, which include Taiwan. Yet for the structure data the resulting distortion is negligible. Total population and share of animal production are from Statistical Yearbook of China 1986, Hongkong 1986: 15 and 130, which do not include Taiwan. Unweighted averages, in approximation derived from CMEA statistical annuals 1981: 191, 1984: 157 and 1987: 169; for Vietnam based on 1975 = 100, for China recalculated from FAO indices.

(b) Only crop and livestock output taken into account, other rural activities (aquatics, 'side line', etc.) excluded.

(c) The FAO figure neglects the effect of multiple cropping. Including it, the sown area in China was 144.2 million hectares in 1984, of which 112.9 sown to grain, see China Agriculture Yearbook 1985, Beijing, 1986: 114, and the yield per hectare 3.6 tonnes. For Vietnam, no figures of multiple cropping are available, but the effect must be yet greater, as the CMEA statistics indicate 8.61 million hectares of sown area, but only 5.62 million of arable land (in 1986).

(d) In calculating land units, a hectare of arable and permanent crop land is assessed at 1.0, one hectare of other agricultural land, basically pasture, at 0.2.

(e) Livestock units are calculated on the basis of one horse and camel = 1.0, one head of cattle and other bovines, including calves = 0.8, one pig = 0.25 and one sheep or goat = 0.1 unit.

(f) For China, excluding potatoes and other tubers; including these at one-quarter to one fifth of their physical weight, the output per head of the population is roughly 390 kg. For Vietnam, the figure is for rice only; including alll other food crops (official equivalents of unhusked rice) it is 292.

(g) Perhaps neglecting the effect of multiple cropping (see (d); for Vietnam the figure is for rice only and much lower for other grains, which occupy a mere 16 per cent of the grain sown land.

(h) For Mongolian grain exports in 1986, FAO data are not available, therefore the balance is only for the 1984–5 two-year average. But the CMEA statistics on Mongolia (which, however, do not give grain imports data) show a doubling of the exports in 1986 on the basis of greatly increased domestic output, so that over the three years exports may have exceeded imports of grain. For Cuba, FAO data are available only on imports of grain, yet if there were exports at all, they must have been negligible and the balance only slightly below 211 kg.

(i) For more realistic figures, see Peter Gey in the present volume (Chapter 4).

(j) No data on state enterprises other than the 9.0 per cent for state farms proper; therefore the rest, which comprises plots and, mainly in South Vietnam, individual peasants, may be less than the 29.6 per cent derived arithmetically.

Sources: Except for China and where not otherwise indicated: CMEA statistical annual *Statisticheskii ezhegodnik stran-chlenov Soveta Ekonomicheskoi Vzaimopomoshchi*, 1987. Moscow 1987: 170–1, 174, 176–7, 193–4, 212, 1988: 202, and 1986: 187–8, 204. Data for land, livestock units, agri culturally active population and grain output per head taken or derived from FAO *Production Yearbook*, Rome, vols. 30 and 40, Tables 1, 2, 3, 4, 15, and FAO *Trade Yearbook* vol. 30, Table 34, and vol. 40, Table 37.

practical significance for countries which liberated themselves, first of all for those among them who chose the way of a socialist orientation. This experience has a special value for the countries neighbouring with Vietnam – the People's Democratic Republic of Laos and the People's Republic of Kambodja. (Quoted from Isaev and Pivovarov 1987: 202)

Yet it remains to be seen whether the recent Vietnamese approach to the peasants and their 'collectivities' (A. Fforde) will herald a sustained policy, which can justify a claim to a model role in Communist agrarian policy, adapted to the special conditions of Southeast Asian paddy rice agriculture. Economic exigency might now enforce continuity, but the past vagaries do not bode too well for such consistency over the longer term. A time-table presents the following picture:[2]

1950–60:   Main period of collectivization of agriculture in North Vietnam (NV).

1960:   86.6 per cent of all peasant families and 76 per cent of all tilled land in NV in collectives, mainly those of the 'lower' types, i.e. not fully collectivized, types.

Early 1970s: 95 per cent of farms and 90 per cent of tilled land in collective farms of the 'higher type', i.e. with full socialization of the means of production, except for plot land and small implements.

End of 1970s: 25.5 per cent of all collective farms 'enlarged', i.e. representing units of the rural commune level.

1977:   Beginnings of 'family contracting' in Haiphong city district (Schmelev, 1987b: 60).

1977:   September: Second CC Plenum formed a commission for the 'transformation' of agriculture in South Vietnam (SV), which was to proceed in stages, the first consisting in the formation of groups of mutual peasant help (fifty to sixty peasants each), in a second step of production brigades of 'lower type' (sixty to eighty peasants and 30–50 hectares), finally collectives, still of a 'lower type' (300–500 hectares). Peasant reluctance/resistance was considerable.

1980:   In Central Vietnam, 83 per cent of farms and 76 per cent of tilled land in production brigades and collective farms. But in SV the 31 per cent of peasant households, which were so organized by 1979, dropped again to 9 per cent with 7 per cent of tilled land by 1980.

1980:   December: The new constitution declares land 'the

property of the people'. This had practical implications mainly for SV as land in NV was already socialized in one way or other.

1981: 'Family contracting' approved by a directive of the Central Committee (CC) of the Communist Party (Schmelev, 1987b: 60).

1982: March: The Fifth Party Congress condemns 'voluntarism' and 'haste' applied in SV collectivization, sets main goals, of which one is to 'solve the food problem' and to 'complete the socialist transformation' of agriculture in SV, but mainly through production brigades. The production goal for the 1981–5 average was set at 17 million tonnes of rice equivalents, which was said to be by 3.5 million tonnes more than the 1976–80 average; for 1990 it was set at 350 kilograms per head, which implies 22–23 million tonnes. (According to CMEA data, the 1981–5 average actually achieved was 16.2 million tonnes.)

1983: May: A CC directive concreticizes the collectivization goal and also mentions that in SV collectivization the 'lower forms' should predominate.

1983: end of year: 'Output contracting' was being applied in 98 per cent of co-operatives in the plain areas of NV and the coastal areas of the central provinces, in 90 per cent of those in SV and 60 per cent of those in the mountain provinces. (Schmelev, 1987b: 60).

Mid–1984: 71.7 per cent of peasants collectivized in SV.

1986: beginning of year: In SV 87.2 per cent of peasants and 85.5 per cent of tilled land collectivized, but, according to Shmelev, in 'various kinds of production brigades', which implies 'lower' forms and output contracting (Schmelev, 1987a: 78)

Similarities and diversity among the four countries

Some general data and indicators of the food economies of the four countries are computed in the Table 1.1. They are, of course, only approximations, based as they are on highly aggregated and in some cases not very reliable data, which are not exactly comparable among the countries. This applies, above all, to the data on the agriculturally active population, in particular with regard to the time per person and year actually worked in agriculture. It is also known that the tilled land area in China is larger by roughly one-third than the statistics indicate. All the same, the approximate contours of the picture are clear enough.

Apart from the differences in size and geographic location and the politically determined farm structure, it immediately emerges from the figures that the Asian socialist countries greatly differ from their European counterparts, but among them (except perhaps for North Korea, on which not enough is known) they share indicators such as: fast growing population (except for China since the late 1970s); high share of agricultural in total economically active population; small share of arable and permanent crop land in total territory; and resulting poor endowment with such land per agricultural worker. Among them, Mongolia differs in having a large share of pasture land and therefore a food production which is essentially based on livestock, whereas in China and Vietnam the intensive crop production, partly based on irrigation, by far dominates. All three managed to keep their dependence on grain imports small. As to the categories of farms, all three were similar in that collective farms had by far the greatest share in land, labour and livestock. China, of course, since the early 1980s has returned to peasant farming on nationalized land, with about five per cent of it occupied by State farms.[3]

In Mongolia much of the immense area of pasture is semi-arid and of very low productivity, and therefore the 'land units' recalculated in Table 1.1 overstate her potential. The numbers of animals are high in absolute terms and also per head of the population, but very low in relation to the land: twenty-four livestock units per 100 hectares of land.

Mongolia's agriculture is heavily involved in foreign trade. The country supplies roughly one-fifth of its meat output to the USSR and at the same time is dependent on Soviet deliveries of crop products and industrial goods. Meat exports are natural for such a country, but the surplus available for export is declining. According to the CMEA statistics, output per head of the population declined from 162 kilograms in 1975 to 120 and 124 in 1985 and 1986 respectively, and in view of the rather constant export quantities of 40,000–50,000 tonnes per year, consumption must have declined yet faster. Presently, Mongolia seems to have become autarkic in grain supplies, but if her population continues to grow at the fast rate, and her livestock production is to be intensified, sizable additional quantities of grain will be needed. On balance, food supplies per head of the Mongolian population have re-attained the level of the mid-1970s only one decade later.

Politically, Mongolia had already been drawn into the Soviet orbit in the early 1920s, but full Soviet-type collectivization started only a quarter of a century later than in the USSR. As distinct from comparable steppe regions of Soviet Asia, where, during the 1930s, the nomads were either made sedentary or turned into half-nomads (transhumance), such a change was up to this time not attempted for the majority of nomads in Mongolia. Thus they were spared the terrible human and material losses of the nomadic tribes in Soviet Central Asia. To arrive at a combination of still basically nomadic forms of livestock raising, as dictated by nature, and a collective way of production and life, as aimed at by the political leaders, which still is economically viable, remains the central problem of Mongolian agrarian policy.

Contrasting the Asian countries, the Cuban indicators in Table 1.1 stand out as being comparable to those of some regions of Eastern Europe and the Soviet Union. Already before the revolution of 1959 Cuba's degree of urbanization and industrialization was higher than in typical underdeveloped countries, but the country pursued a policy of further rapid industrialization. The population growth during the past ten to fifteen years was much slower than in Vietnam and Mongolia (and China up to 1978) and therefore was exceeded by the otherwise modest overall food output growth (including sugar for export). All the same, the demand for food in Cuba exceeds supplies at given (State-fixed) prices, and some foods continue being rationed.

The food economy as well as the overall economy of Cuba are heavily dependent on agricultural foreign trade. The island is the world's biggest exporter of cane sugar and in exchange imports not only industrial goods but also most of the grain it needs and some other basic foods. The policy of producing and exporting sugar and importing grain, while two-thirds of the sown area is devoted to feed crops for increasing animal production, is feasible and makes economic sense only due to the purchases of Cuban sugar by the Soviet Union and other CMEA countries at prices several times higher than those of the world market. Similarly, Castro's utopian agrarian and other domestic policies, as well as his foreign policy, would hardly be possible without such Soviet and CMEA economic assistance, which is conditioned upon various factors, among them Cuba's geopolitical strategic location.

The country deviates from the common pattern also in that the state farm sector is by far dominant. In 1981, production co-operatives and private producers (peasants, plot holders and non-peasants) owned only 4 and 15 per cent, respectively, of the total land. (The CMEA source for Table 1.1 is misleading on that account.) It is only since then that the concept of production co-operatives has been applied to some degree by considerably accelerating the transformation of private farms into co-operatives. Both, however, are rigidly incorporated in the State procurement system. Socialization of agriculture in Cuba has from the beginning focused on the formation of a conglomerate of State enterprises on the basis of pre-existing capitalist large-scale farms.

Communist agrarian reform under different conditions

What the four countries have in common, apart from being ruled by Marxist-Leninist parties, is the lagging of food production behind the aspirations of an industrializing and urbanizing and at the same time growing population. This made itself more and more felt by the end of the 1970s and was the main driving force behind the attempts at reform made since then. Up to roughly that time one finds in all of them a forceful policy of socializing agriculture and of industrialization, mainly based on heavy industry, with a rise in monetary labour incomes among its results.

Food supplies have not generally remained below the physiological minimum requirements, but periodically and regionally there still was severe malnutrition in China and Vietnam. As the Vietnamese newspaper *People's Army* put it on 22 December 1983 with a view to the country's average output of rice equivalents: 'A production of 300 kg per head represents the boundary between penury and temporary [*sic*] sufficiency' (quoted from Isaev and Pivovarov 1987: 178). At that time and most likely even today, this level was not achieved in many provinces of Vietnam, but has been surpassed in China. For Mongolia and Cuba the problem is not one of malnutrition, but of demand for specific foods exceeding supply, which makes itself particularly felt, if over a number of years the majority of a population does not see the expected – and promised! – improvement.

Especially in Mongolia the change from heavy predominance of animal products to an increasing share of crop products was accompanied by virtual stagnation in overall food consumption per head for a decade, and in Cuba the problem 'only' was one of monetary demand exceeding physical food supply. The demand–supply discrepancy was exacerbated by insufficient supplies of attractive non-food consumer goods, on which the monetary incomes might be spent.

Cuba's problems and the level of industrialization are more similar to Eastern Europe than to those of the Far Eastern socialist countries, and compared to other Latin American countries, Cuba shows better in some respects. Yet one has to take into account the fact that it enjoyed the special advantage of an assured and high-price Soviet and East European market for her sugar export and of additional subsidies, in particular Soviet financial and technical aid.

Making the point here that similar problems exist in many non-communist countries of the world, although in somewhat different forms, would miss the essential fact that communist regimes pretend to have better solutions for them and that socializing agriculture is one of their central recipes. Moreover, the FAO indexes of food production per head in the Asian centrally planned economies, as compared to the developing market economies of the Far East, show the former so clearly lagging towards the late 1970s, per head as well as in absolute terms, that the inevitable inaccuracies of such figures are not likely to change the picture fundamentally.

The pressure of food demand exceeding supply had accumulated in non-European as well as European countries under Marxist-Leninist regimes (Hungary and, with qualifications, Bulgaria being the exceptions). One would be hard put to find some other explanation for this parallelism than the socio-economic policies of these very regimes. Marxist-Leninist thought had envisaged only superficial differentiation by countries on the way to the socialist and industrial society, and its more or less uniform implementation in practice had run these into grave difficulties, which also were more or less uniform.

By the late 1970s, a sizably increasing growth rate of agricultural production had become urgent in the three Asian communist countries. In a State-controlled and centrally planned economy, improving the economic performance necessarily implies a change of agrarian policy. And this is what happened rather radically in China and Vietnam, to a certain degree also in Mongolia (as was outlined above for China and will be shown in the chapters on Vietnam and Mongolia). This change consisted in an adaptation to given constraints and exigencies by forsaking, at least for the time being, the preference for large-scale socialist farms. To this end, Marxist-Leninist ideology had to be pragmatically re-interpreted to a degree, which would have seemed unthinkable a decade earlier. This was done most radically in China, to a remarkable degree in Vietnam and in a rather conservative way in Mongolia, where in the practice of nomadic animal farming the family had never fully lost its role as the basic production unit.

A parallel process can be observed in the Soviet Union and, to varying degrees, in Eastern Europe with Hungary in the avant-garde, other countries trying more conservative ways, and the Soviet Union embarking on the perestroika course a few years later. Yet the solutions sought were different. To speak of imitation or mutual recommendations appears misleading. Selective adoption of individual features of successful or promising reform seems plausible, but it is no less plausible that similar features may emerge independently from similar circumstances.

If, for example, one considers that for every hectare of tilled land the USSR has roughly twenty times less agricultural workers than China, but several times more capital input, then it looks unlikely that the Chinese 'family responsibility system' can be meaningfully implemented all over the USSR. This does not prohibit its adoption with some modifications, in particular for certain regions. In fact, already the underlying idea of the Soviet 'normless link' of the 1960s was not far from the 1979 and 1980 beginnings of the 'responsibility system' in China before it generally turned to the family as its cornerstone. But when in May, 1988 at the Moscow Agricultural Lenin-Academy president A.A. Nikonov, who is a partisan of 'family links' and 'tenancy contracting', was asked whether something resembling the present Chinese version of the system could be imagined for the oasis agriculture of Soviet Central Asia with its labour surplus and intensive cultivation, this was flatly denied, perhaps mainly for reasons of political principle. On the other hand, similarities of livestock raising in the vast dry steppes of Kazakhstan and Mongolia must not necessarily come about as an imitation, but might as well arise out of comparable natural conditions and working traditions in those two vast areas. Twenty years ago at the Institute of Karakul Sheep Raising at Samarkand I was told that the brigades in the dry steppes sheep farms of Uzbekistan in actual fact consisted of extended families.

It seems self-evident that among numerous and manifold factors determining policy decisions, the inclinations of the political leadership, including their fear of rocking the boat of the established power structure too much, does not range in the last place. This factor is hard to assess, however, and leaves much room for informed prognostication by the political scientist and psychologist. At any rate, it may be stated that in the long run, in a sequence of successors, dogmatic political leadership can act in total independence of economic and social conditions only at the price of self-defeat. By the end of the 1970s even the Cubans embarked on a kind of rationalization of the running of their economy, including some tolerance for private farming and food markets. This was reversed in 1986, but the question seems legitimate whether Fidel Castro could have afforded his erratic return to revolutionary romanticism, if the Cuban economy were not kept afloat by the privileged sugar exports and the Soviet subsidies. Relying on them may be called a Cuban brand of pragmatism, but surely is of a very specific vintage not available to others.

The more a rational kind of pragmatism imposes itself on agricultural policy, the more it must take into consideration the economic and sociopolitical circumstances in very different countries and also regions. Leninist-Marxist ideology in its Stalinist form without pragmatism forced Russian agriculture into the Prokrustes bed of the kolkhoz system, but the price was inefficiency and decay in most of historical Russia. With the spreading of the ideological policy beyond the Soviet borders, the price had to be paid in ever greater parts of the hegemonial sphere. This became yet more obvious when this sphere encompassed totally different agrarian countries of Asia.

It was by the late 1970s that it became inevitable for the ideology pragmatically to adapt to given conditions of agricultural production, that is, to embark on a process of change which has begun to transgress what once was considered unswerving Marxist-Leninist orthodoxy. The process continues and is fascinating for observers of socialized agriculture, most of all with regard to China, but also to a wide range of cases in the majority of countries under communist regimes. It is intriguing to see, why and in which ways Marxist-Leninist agrarain policy and the underlying ideology have been and will further be forced to adapt to the widely differing conditions in the countries where it established its rule and wants to maintain it, and thereby is likely to develop in different directions. Concentrating only on Eastern Europe and the Soviet Union would deprive us of a broader understanding of the variety of processes.

Notes

1. I wish to thank Claude Aubert in Paris, and Günther Jaehne in Giessen, for valuable comments on, and help with, an earlier draft of this introductory chapter. Responsibility for misjudgements in facts or interpretation rests, of course, with me.
2. Where not otherwise indicated, the subsequent data are from Isaev and Pivovarov, 1987: 81–2, 89, 119, 133–5, 137, 145, 148–9, 154, 171, 174, 181.
3. The only thorough Western study on Chinese state farms, to this writer's knowledge, is the printed dissertation by Richard Gerhold, *Staatsgüter in der Volksrepublik China*, Giessen and Berlin (West), 1987.

References

Isaev, M.P., Pivovarov, la N. (1987) *Ocherk agrarnykh otnoshenii*, Moscow.
Schmelev, G.I. (1987a) *Sem'ia beret podriad*, Moscow.
Schmelev, G.I. (1987b) *Sem'ia v sfere proizvodstva*, Moscow.

Chapter two

The 'Chinese model' and the future of rural-urban development

Claude Aubert

Introduction

The agricultural reforms in China turned the workers of the previous People's Communes into autonomous peasants on collectively owned land, and greatly raised labour productivity on farms. Thereby hidden agricultural underemployment became an open and officially acknowledged problem. Concomitantly, the reforms lifted most, though not all, restrictions on peasants' economic activities and domicile, they encouraged the undertaking of numerous non-agricultural activities and so induced the rise in the number of market towns which is the major event of the mid-1980s in the Chinese countryside.

Even if one can hesitate to qualify such a development as a decisive move towards a real urbanization, it is above debate that such a change has thoroughly modified the rural situation, creating almost 50 million new non-agricultural jobs within six years, thereby relieving the prevalent underemployment in Chinese villages (which has not completely disappeared). It is intimately connected with the development of labour productivity in agriculture, rural incomes and the development of interregional markets.

The future of this development remains questionable. Indeed, more jobs can be created in the tertiary sector in small towns, but the future growth of rural industry is anything but sure, with the exception of the economically advanced coastal areas of East China where such industry

16

is already developing in osmosis with existing great cities, more than with local agriculture. In a way, one wonders whether the past fast rise of non-agricultural activities in the countryside and the multiplication of market-towns and small towns, are not simply the catching-up of their past backward state, since decades of authoritarian controls restricted any rural or agricultural exodus.

Then one cannot consider as entirely reasonable the official hopes of the Chinese way for progressive urbanization, axed on the priority development of small towns and rural industry, avoiding a massive rural exodus and the congestion of big cities. One cannot exclude, if police controls are further relaxed, that massive migrations from the countryside to the cities may occur in the future. For the time being the exodus is still mainly 'agricultural', with workers commuting between their village families and the town workshops where they work for the main part of the year. But the rural exodus has already started: since 1982, 10 million people have migrated to the towns or to the cities every year. The big cities are no longer spared, they number many temporary workers from the villages employed in construction projects, housework, etc. In 1986, these numbered 1 million persons in Peking, 1.6 million in Shanghai. For the whole of China, these emigrated peasants, still registered in their former villages, but living and working most of the year in the great cities, were estimated at 6 million persons in 1984, and up to 20 million in 1985.

The threat of a massive rural exodus is still not for today, but it already worries the Chinese authorities: such an exodus would question one of the very basic tenets of the present political regime which, up to now, has never ceased to protect the class interest of workers and employees in the State sectors. This threat divides Chinese economists and policy makers, who do not agree on the desirable future mode of urbanization and, therefore, on the necessary control of population migrations. The economists are divided too in their opinions regarding the development of a small rural capitalism, based on family industries and services, still a minority in rural China, but fast growing and competing with collective enterprises.

The outcome to be hoped for is that, together with an accelerated but measured rural exodus, the rural industry may continue to grow, free from administrative interference, and thus becoming the starting point for the development of the countryside as well as of the whole Chinese economy. The worst, unfortunately, cannot be excluded too. Would it be a quick exhaustion of the present rise of rural enterprises and market-towns; or an out of control massive rural exodus conducive to an urban maldevelopment observed elsewhere in other under-developed countries; or, last but not least, a return to police controls blocking any more evolutions.

Even if the turning point of the last years did not result in so rapid an urbanization progress as suggested by the official set of figures, the evolution has been profound and real enough to completely modify the features of the rural sector. This change could even be decisive for the future of the whole Chinese economy.

Urbanization and rural–urban migrations

During the years 1979–82, under the ambiguous cover of the responsibility systems, the Chinese authorities undertook the silent revolution of a true decollectivization in the countryside (for a short summary of the preceding agrarian policies, see Chapter 1). At the end of 1984, when the 'People's Communes' began to fade out of the official terminology, a *de facto* privatization of agriculture was already under way. In the same manner, the State monopolies on the agricultural products marketing were abolished in 1985. At that time, the whole system of compulsory procurements had already been diverted from its original purpose during several years, by the use of multiple prices and by the growing importance of 'above quota' sales in the peasants' deliveries (Aubert, 1982, 1984, 1985).

After the breath-taking changes of the early 1980s, the countryside now appears very quiet. The only news is that of the first set-backs of the reforms which seem to have exhausted their own capacity for economic revival: drop of the grain output following the miraculous harvest of the immediate post-decollectivization period (Aubert, 1986a),[1] spreading of black market activities along the villages that nobody controls anymore. . . . However, a new evolution, no less revolutionary than the past return to household agriculture, is now silently taking place. According to the well-known demographer Judith Banister, of the US Bureau of Census, China is now going through an accelerated urbanization process, contrasting with decades of urban stagnation. The inhabitants of towns and cities, which made up 21 per cent of the total population in 1982, would have reached 37 per cent in 1986 . . . and should probably exceed 50 per cent by the turn of the century (Banister and Woodard, 1987)! So a vast array of new towns are supposed to be booming in the Chinese countryside.

If these facts were confirmed, they would mean a very important change indeed, after more than five centuries of uninterrupted ruralization in the Chinese historical development (this change would be noteworthy too, in the sense that it would be impulsed by the growth of a small rural capitalism). The flourishing of a great many new towns seems to be related to the creation of innumerable private rural enterprises, regulated by market economics. Then a new urban, capitalist, structure would seem to encircle the old cities, which remain the core of socialist economics. This new version of the encircling of the cities by the countryside would be very ironical after the past theories of the late Mao Zedong and Lin Biao. At least, it would constitute an entirely new situation with far-reaching implications both for the coming development of China and for the future of its political regime. But, what is really going on?

The official figures seem to confirm Judith Banister's statements. According to the last set of figures published by the Chinese Statistical Yearbook (Table 2.1, Urb. pop. (1)), the percentage of urban within total population, after stagnating at 17–18 per cent during the 1960s and 1970s, had gone beyond the 20 per cent mark in 1981, and reached 35.6 per cent at the end of 1985.

It is not sure, however, that the urbanization rate is really as high as suggested by these official figures. 'Urban population' figures, in China as elsewhere, depend on employed definitions, and in China these varied at different times, giving place to a variety of interpretations. (For the statistical technicalities of the calculations involved and the author's own estimations, the reader is referred to the Appendix 2.1).

Two available, and in themselves consistent, sets of urban population figures – 'total urban' and/or 'non-agricultural' urban – emerge from our calculations, but only the latter, so it seems, can reflect, with reasonable probability, the true degree of urbanization in China. And this degree is much lower than the one implied by Banister's calculations: a level of only 12 per cent urban people in the total population in 1976 made China a massively rural country, well behind India, at that time. The degree of 18 per cent reached in 1985 meant only a return to a more normal situation, considering the level of development then attained by China.

The backward state of urbanization of the 1960s and 1970s was not the effect of spontaneous development, but resulted from a deliberate policy, having at its disposition powerful bureaucratic and police instruments. This fact is well-demonstrated by the analysis of urban-rural migrations that we can now undertake (Table 2.5). We have reconstructed, in great detail, all these migrations from 1952 to 1985, using the calculations made by Kirby (1985) on natural urban growth rates with some corrections and a more precise periodization.

It is possible to distinguish six different phases during this whole period, with distinct patterns of migrations (considering only non-agricultural urban versus rural population).

1. The years from 1952 to 1957 present a quick urbanization process of accelerated industrialization under the auspices of the First Five-Year Plan: of the 12 million new rural persons resulting each year from natural demographic growth, about four million, one third, are migrating to the towns.
2. The second phase, 1957–1960, corresponds to the 'Great Leap

Forward' which disproportionately inflated the towns with an enormous exodus, reaching 15 million people in the peak year of 1959.

3. The economic collapse which resulted from the Great Leap's follies, with millions of deaths by famine, is accompanied by a drastic reduction in the urban population by the authoritarian sending back to their villages of millions of newly immigrated peasants: 32 million persons were so driven out of the cities by force, during this third phase (1960–4).

4. At the beginning of the fourth, and longest phase, 1964–76, the degree of urbanization is then back to its 1957 level. It will slowly go down throughout this period, with a net total outflow from the cities of five million people. This outflow masks, however, a small but real rural exodus from the villages into the towns, if we are to consider that 17 million young people were forcibly sent to the countryside after graduating from city schools: 1 million peasants, during each of these twelve years, were then discreetly pouring into the cities, a very small exodus indeed, compared to the natural demographic growth of 18 million new rural people annually.

5. During the fifth phase, 1976–82, this exodus increases its momentum with 3 million peasants migrating each year to the cities, while most of the 'educated young youths', previously sent to the countryside, returned to their urban homes after the death of Mao Zedong (1976).

6. The final phase, 1982–5, shows a real turning point, the rural exodus increasing threefold, up to near 10 million people each year, more then than the demographic growth in the countryside.

The magnitude of the migrational variations, their very changes of orientation, are the proof of the immense importance of authoritarian controls of population flows, at least when Mao Zedong was still alive. The main instrument of these controls has been, and still is, the 'hukou' system of police registration of residents who cannot change their domiciliation at will (which is, for most of the male peasants, their birthplace). This fixing of the population in their living places was complemented, until a recent date, by a strict rationing of food grain in the cities, and prohibition of its sales on the free markets, complemented, too, by the peasants being forbidden to travel without proper authorization (Kirby, 1985: 21–53).

These formidable tools for population control gave power enough to the authorities for sending back to their villages those peasants who emigrated to the cities during the Great Leap Forward, for sending to the countryside millions of young educated urban people, and, above all, for interrupting almost completely any rural exodus of significant size during the major part of the 1960s and 1970s.

During all this period, the urban structure practically did not change.

The population distribution in cities above 100,000 inhabitants remained almost the same from 1953 to 1982 (Table 2.4): with the major part occupied by the big cities of 1 million persons and more (almost half the total city population), a lesser part for medium-size cities (one-third of the total for those between 0.3 and 1 million persons), and a minor part for small cities (less than 0.3 million persons). The proportion of the small towns' population within the total urban population also remained stable at about 30 per cent.

The renewal of the rural exodus at the end of the 1970s, and its present acceleration, are the clear indication of a progressive removal of past authoritarian controls. Peasants now have the right to settle definitively in the small towns (according to a 1984 circular, and this explains the booming of these small towns during 1985 and 1986). They may travel as they want for business or work purposes (without the right, however, to change their *hukou* registration). The State monopoly on retail sales of foodgrain has been abolished (Aubert, 1985). All these changes have considerably lightened the controls on migrations without suppressing them completely. They were the unescapable counterpart of the agricultural reforms which occurred after the death of Mao Zedong, with the return on the political scene of the pragmatical reformists to power in Peking. The coming back of less-constrained migratory flows have given way to a more balanced structure of the urban population. The great cities, the access to which remains tightly controlled, have lost some of their relative importance, giving more weight to the small and medium cities (Table 2.4). More important, the small towns have known an unprecedented growth, passing from 30 per cent of the total non-agricultural urban population to almost 40 per cent (Table 2.3).

An overpopulated countryside

Considering the inversion of trends in the last years, due to the agricultural reforms of the late 1970s, we must divide the evolution of the countryside into successive stages that we propose to compare and oppose: the collectivization stage, ending in the summer of 1978 where its purest, orthodox, phase is concerned (Third Plenum of the Eleventh CCP Congress, having ratified the change of policies in December 1978); a stage of more liberal policies in the countryside, with the decollectivization process of 1979–82; and the evolutions that followed.

The first period – collectivization –may be characterized as a time of true 'agricultural involution,[2] if we consider its performances, measured between the years 1957 and 1976.

To be sure, the agricultural production increased by a big margin from 1957 to 1976. Grain harvests went up by 50 per cent, from 191 million tonnes to 286 million tonnes, with an annual growth rate of 3.5 per cent from 1964 to 1976, and a doubling of yields for wheat and corn (TJNJ, 1986: 174–80). The gross value of total agricultural output increased by 50 per cent too, most of the progression occurring after the recovery of the early 1960s, following the Great Leap disaster. The twelve years between 1964 and 1976 were precisely those of the 'Green Revolution' then spreading all over the Chinese countryside.

Did labour productivity rise accordingly during all this period?

In order to measure this productivity, first one has to estimate the exact number of agricultural workers at that time. The official bureau of statistics gives us two sets of figures (that we had to make up for a few missing years): one concerns the total rural manpower (both collective and individual, belonging to the country population of communes or townships), the other numbers only the agricultural labourers (Table 2.6, columns Rural Labor and Agricultural Labor). This last one includes many seasonal workers in the village industries, so we established another set of figures (Table 2.6. Estimated agricultural labour) with only genuine peasants, their number being arrived at by subtracting the total number of workers in rural non-agricultural enterprises and the employees in the education, health, and administration sectors from the total rural manpower.

Assessed per agricultural worker, the performances of the collectivized agriculture appear definitely not so bright. The annual grain production per full-time worker did not progress significantly during the whole period (0.99 tonne in 1957, 1.03 tonne in 1976), while other productions collapsed (8.5 kg of ginned cotton, 21.7 kg of oil-seeds per worker in 1957, only 7.4 and 14 kg respectively in 1976) (TJNJ, 1986: 174–86). The gross value of agricultural production per labourer increased by a small margin, from 112 (index 100 in 1952) to 117 (Table 2.7), but this progress is not meaningful as one should deduct the increased value of industrial inputs, used on a big scale at the end of the period (5.77 million tonnes of chemical fertilizers, effective nutrients, employed in 1976, against 370,000 tonnes in 1957). A more adequate assessment of the rural sector's productivity can be found in the agricultural revenue aggregate (net of production expenses, but including the revenues of village industries): divided by the official number of agricultural workers (then including those of the village industry), this agricultural revenue fell from 1957 to 1976 (index 108 in 1957, 100 in 1976).

This stagnation, even regression, of the agricultural productivity of labour, in spite of the overall expansion of agriculture, clearly manifests the existence of a real involution. This involution is also characterized by a lack of diversification in the production, with the official policy stressing the priority for grain production all along (the cultivated surface for industrial crops remained stagnant from 1957 to 1976, with only

9 per cent of the total cropped area) (TJNJ, 1986: 174), and the fall of non-agricultural revenues in the peasants' earnings. Measured through a representative sample of peasant families in the Hubei province, the proportion of these non-agricultural revenues fell from 15 per cent in 1954, to 11 per cent in 1964 . . . and only 6 per cent in 1974 (Table 2.8).

This involution was also concomitant with a retracting, a growing autarky of the Chinese countryside. The commercialized part of the agricultural production, which reached 43 per cent in 1957, was no more than 39 per cent in 1976. During the same time, the gross procurements of grain fell from 25 per cent of the harvest to 20 per cent only (Table 2.5).

We do not intend to analyse here the numerous factors of such an involution, particularly the use of low administrative prices for the quota of compulsory deliveries which depressed the overall production and discouraged peasant sales. We want to emphasize one particularly important factor – a central one in our present discussion on urban-rural relationships – which is the growing rural overpopulation within the context of a strict control of any migration.

The paradox in China is that the agricultural manpower increased by 86 million people (193 million workers in 1957, 279 million in 1976), while mechanical equipment was much more numerous in the countryside: there were only 15,000 tractors in 1957, but 1.2 million (tractors and motor-cultivators) in 1976; the mechanical irrigation equipment totalled 0.6 million horsepower in 1957, 54 million in 1976 (NYNJ, 1980: 39) etc. In these conditions, there is nothing strange that the tractors were used for transportation and not for field cultivation.

The available agricultural manpower was already quite numerous at the beginning of the period (1.7 agricultural workers per cultivated hectare in 1957), it became superabundant (2.8 workers per hectare in 1976), while the rural exodus was interrupted after the massive sending of new immigrants back to the villages in the early 1960s (see above). The collective structures of production gave the authorities an efficient tool for controlling population flows by organizing the daily activities of the peasants, preventing any unauthorized move to the cities. Moreover, the workforce mobilized for collective tasks was not permitted to undertake off-season private non-agricultural activities at all, as it used to in the past, within families; hence the drop in the non-agricultural revenues cf the peasants' earnings as observed in the province of Hubei. On the other hand, the collective organization of agricultural work facilitated the absorption, in its totality, of the whole agricultural labour force available in the countryside – at the price of declining labour productivity.

This massive absorption of manpower in the collectivized agricultural sector masked a growing underemployment. Of course, it is extremely difficult to assess the labour surplus which then resulted, and which the collectives employed without consequent rise in production or economic efficiency. Chinese authorities, afterwards, estimated that this surplus reached, at the end of the 1970s, between one-third to one-half of the total rural manpower, i.e. 100 to 150 million people who were unnecessarily employed in agricultural tasks and should have been more usefully employed elsewhere. These enormous figures have been corroborated by (apparently) more scientific calculations by Chinese economists (Li QZ, 1986; Liu ZP, 1987).

However, this very notion of labour surplus is questionable, and quite relative as a large part of these not fully occupied workers are in fact necessary for peak season agricultural tasks. A better approach to this disguised underemployment may be found in the precise analysis of agricultural labour requirements for different crops.

During the autumn of 1981, some personal investigations were made in several provinces of China in order to establish, on the basis of interviews of peasants and within the technology then employed, the number of labour days really required for the main crops. Using quite generous standards (often double those previously observed in Taiwanese villages using the same technology), the following figures were obtained: 80 man-work days for cultivating one hectare of wheat, 90 days for corn, 200 days for one crop of rice (Aubert, 1981). Of course, these were average figures, allowing, in practice, for great variation from place to place, and they merely indicate some kind of order of magnitude for the work involved. These figures were already higher than those observed by J. L. Buck, fifty years before, in the same Chinese provinces: 50 days for wheat and corn, 120 days for rice (Buck, 1937). Thus, the gain in work time obtained from the mechanization of irrigation was more than offset by the intensification of agricultural tasks for field management (fertilization, weeding, and so on), as the ploughing and harvesting were still not mechanized. Although these labour requirements are, deliberately, slightly overestimated, and anyway higher than those observed by Buck, they were, nevertheless, lower by a large margin than the number of days which had been paid to the peasants for the same crops by the cadres of the collectives in the late 1970s, before the decollectivization process. In 1976, for the whole of China, these figures were: 450 work days for one hectare of wheat or corn, 600 days for rice (NYSC, 1984: 642–4)! Even if we note that these numbers were recorded for accounting purposes, and may be higher than the number of days actually worked by peasants (a strong labourer may get one-and-a-half, even two days' pay for one real work day), the difference with our own estimations of labour requirements is so big (a ratio of 1:5

for wheat and corn, 1:3 for rice) that we cannot avoid the conclusion that there was, at that time, a massive underemployment, a frightening mis-utilization of manpower in the countryside, disguised under the full employment achieved by the agricultural collectives.

These inflated work times, this wastage of manpower have been the direct counterpart of the prohibitions to the workers, both for migrating to the cities and for undertaking non-agricultural private ventures. As a consequence, with the aggravation of such under-employment coupled with the widening of the prices' scissors of agricultural versus industrial prices (Aubert, 1985), the gap between the standard of living in the overcrowded villages, and the one of town-dwellers, well-protected within their urban strongholds, never ceased to deepen. In 1964, at the very beginning of this long period of accentuated ruralization in China, city-dwellers' daily life expenses totalled 221 yuans per person and per year, while for peasants this figure was 95 yuans (self-consumption included), i.e. a ratio of 2.33:1. In 1978, the respective figures were 365 and 116 yuans, i.e. a ratio of 3.15:1 (TJNJ, 1986: 668–74; ZGMYWJ, 1984).

Productivity effects of decollectivization and raised prices

From 1978 on, the agricultural reforms fortunately interrupted this vicious circle of agricultural involution and the degradation of peasants' life conditions. These reforms have had successive effects that we must differentiate.

The decollectivization, achieved in 1982, induced improved efficiency for labour, thereafter mobilized within household farms. To this increase in efficiency was added the stimulation of upgraded agricultural prices, as the State could not go on buying at low prices the surpluses of the decollectivized agriculture. The prices soared up at an unprecedented pace; the average index for all types of procurement prices, which was 100 in 1957 and only 149 in 1978, went up to 211 in 1982 and 248 in 1985 (TJNJ, 1986: 624). So, the prices increased by 66 per cent during the seven years from 1978 to 1985, against a mere 49 per cent for the previous twenty years of collectivized agriculture.

The new motivations for the peasants, autonomous in their individual farms and responding to price incentives, resulted in big production increases. Grain witnessed miracle harvests during the years of the immediate post-decollectivization, with an average annual growth of almost 5 per cent from 1978 to 1984. The industrial crops, now rehabilitated and benefiting from advantageous relative prices, boomed fantastically, recovering their past importance: cotton harvests tripled from 1976 to 1984, as did oilseed between 1978 and 1985.

Of course, these true great leaps forward in production affected positively the labour productivity which again began to progress, after the stagnation or regression during the collectivization years. Grain production for each agricultural worker, which stagnated a long time at the one tonne mark, reached 1.36 tonne in 1984. Certainly, the gross value of agricultural production per worker (calculated at constant prices) almost doubled from 1976 to 1985 (respective indices 117 and 197), but we also have to take into account the doubling of the inputs during the same period (5.8 million tonnes of chemical fertilizers used in 1976, 17.8 million in 1985) (see TJNJ, 1986: 149).[3] A more accurate indictor, the 'agricultural revenue per worker', which corresponds to a net value of agricultural production, shows, and for the first time, a real take-off: increasing by 64 per cent from 1976 to 1985 (constant prices) (Table 2.7).

Peasant sales, too, were booming, putting an end to the past vicious circle of growing autarky. The commercialization rate increased from 39 per cent in 1976 to 51 per cent in 1985 with a growing importance of the free market (less than 5 per cent of total sales in 1976, almost 17 per cent in 1985) (Table 2.9).

These first effects of the reforms, renewal of efficiency in the household farms, renewed price incentives, now seem, however, to be rapidly exhausting themselves. After the record harvest of 1984, the grain production fell in 1985 and did not recover its record level in 1986. In the same year 1986, it was the turn of cotton and oilseed production to drop (RMRB, 22 February 1987). In fact, the uninterrupted increase of agricultural prices, from 1978 on, cannot be maintained any longer. And the problem of prices is further aggravated by the difficulties of the new market regulation of agricultural production which has been progressively substituted for the past authoritarian planification of compulsory deliveries (Aubert, 1986b).

In this context of slowing agricultural growth, labour productivity, however, did not stop improving. After 1984, the first effects of agricultural reforms have been taken over by another consequence of the structural changes, somewhat delayed and masked by the spectacular evolutions of the early 1980s, but none the less decisive for the future: the decrease, both in absolute and relative numbers, of agricultural manpower.

This decrease appears clearly in our set of estimates for the numbers of agricultural workers, which after a peak of 309 million people in 1983, never ceased to go down thereafter, already under the 300 million mark at the end of 1985 (Table 2.6). During the reforms of the late 1970s and early 1980s the proportion of agricultural workers in the total rural manpower did not change and remained at the high level of 90 per cent; now, it has dropped suddenly to 89 per cent in 1985 (or 60 per cent only of the total manpower, whether rural or not, of China).

This turning point is not due to massive migrations to the cities, even if it occurs at the same time as the rise of the rural exodus we noted for 1982 on. In fact, despite this acceleration of the rural exodus, manpower in the townships[4] went on growing during the last years, maintaining a stable rate of about 74–75 per cent of the total workforce of China (Table 2.6). The migrations to the towns, exceeding the natural demographic growth in the countryside, could not offset the coming on the labour market of millions of young peasants, born during the baby-boom of 1963–9 and highly mobilized in the family farms: the rate of working people in the rural population rose from 38 per cent in 1978 to 44 per cent in 1985.

The new fact is the turning of a growing part of the rural population to non-agricultural activities. The manpower of rural non-agricultural enterprises tripled between 1980 and 1985, from 25 million people to 75 million, most of this expansion having taken place after 1983 (RMRB, 4 June 1987). It is precisely this massive increase of non-agricultural workers (who may return to the fields in agricultural peak seasons) which induced the booming of market-towns which happened after 1982.

The mere question of defining these new market-towns as urban or not urban may not be, after all, an important one. The point is to stress the decisive importance of the change in the structure of occupations in the countryside. Such a change occurring now is indeed coming to the forefront after the structural reforms of labour organization (the decollectivization) and product commercialization (the ending of State monopolies).

This recent move is, quite obviously, the direct consequence of the decollectivization process, as peasants needed to regain their decision-making autonomy in order to be free to take up their off season non-agricultural activities. It is also the result of government's political will, with the promulgation in 1984, by the State Council and Party Central Committee of two circulars (Nos 1 and 4) which proved to be crucial: they permitted the peasants to settle in the small towns for work, they eased the administrative procedures for the creation of new workshops and services, they opened new credit lines for business, etc. (Shen LR, 1985).

Such a diversification of rural activities, combined with the rise in agricultural prices, was instrumental in narrowing the gap between standards of living in cities and villages. In 1985, the annual daily-life expenditure per person was 732 yuans for city dwellers against 317 yuans for villagers, i.e. a ratio of 2.3:1 (TJNJ, 1986: 668–73); this ratio had been 3.15:1 in 1978. Of the peasants' earnings, non-agricultural revenues (measured through our Hubei sample) increased from 6 per cent in 1974 to 23 per cent in 1985 (Table 2.8).

Of course, the rise in peasants' revenues (133 yuans per person per year in 1978, to 424 yuans in 1986) (TJNJ, 1986: 673) is partly nominal.

The retail price inflation, much higher than the officially stated 4 per cent annual rate from 1978 to 1985 (TJNJ, 1986: 624), eroded the new purchasing power which appeared during the last years. Moreover, a large part consisted of self-consumption. However, one must admit that standards of living are much better now than during the late 1970s, even if growing disparities make the whole picture somewhat confused. Peasants, on the average, have never eaten so well, with a calorie intake now close to 2,500 calories, with a current annual consumption of 12 kg of meat per head against only 6 kg in 1978 (Aubert, 1985). The rise in purchasing power is patent too with the acquisition of durable consumer goods in great quantities: in 1985, for every 100 peasant families, there were 81 bicycles against 31 in 1978, 43 sewing-machines against 20, 54 radio sets against 17, 126 wrist-watches against 27, and 12 TV sets against zero (in the cities the corresponding figures in 1985 were: 164 bicycles, 73 sewing-machines, 81 radio sets, 287 wrist-watches, and 93 TV sets) (TJNJ, 1986: 669, 676).

To the year 2000: small towns or big cities?

The upgrading of the standard of living in the countryside does not mean that the peasants may soon overtake the city dwellers in the pursuit of economic well-being.

In fact, the level of urbanization reached in China at the end of 1985 (18 per cent for the non-agricultural urban population, or 11 per cent excluding towns of less than 100,000 persons), as well the share of the non-agricultural rural workforce (20 per cent of the total rural manpower) and that of non-agricultural revenues in peasant earnings (23 per cent in Hubei) are quite the same as those observed in the past in other Asian countries of comparable level of development: 14 per cent of urban dwellers in towns of over 100,000 inhabitants for South Asia in 1980, 20 per cent of non-agricultural workers in rural manpower in India during 1966–7, 23 per cent of non-agricultural revenues in the peasant earnings in Pakistan in 1968 (Ho, 1986; Hauser and Gardiner, 1980), etc.

The overpopulation of the Chinese countryside has not disappeared altogether. The agricultural workers' pressure on the cultivated land has increased, from 2.8 workers per hectare in 1976 to 3 workers in 1985. However, the diversification of rural activities has considerably relieved the prevailing underemployment. From 1976 to 1982, the number of work days for each hectare of crops, officially registered, diminished from 450 to 265 for wheat, from 450 to 280 for corn, from 600 days to 380 for rice (Li YZ, 1986). In 1985, the corresponding numbers reported in the province of Hubei (that we surveyed in the autumn of 1986) were no more than 240 days for wheat and 310 days for rice. These work times are still higher than our estimated requirements, but, anyway, they declined by about half their peak level of the collectivization years.

We may, therefore, consider that, in a way, the present situation in rural employment constitutes a return to the norms of other comparable underdeveloped countries, with persisting underemployment, after the abnormal peak levels observed during the period of collective farming.

What lies in the future? Will the present evolution go on, with a continuing expansion of the big market-towns and a true take-off of the rural industry relieving the population pressure on agricultural activities? Or will this rise exhaust itself, so raising the acute question of the proper way for industrialization – and urbanization – to really pull China out of its present state of underdevelopment? This question both preoccupies and divides the Chinese economists.

Official projections for rural employment to the year 2000 are quite optimistic. It is officialy considered that, at that time, total rural manpower will reach the 450 million mark, 50 per cent of whom (i.e. 225 million workers, including 135 million cultivators and 90 million workers in pig-breeding, aquaculture, afforestation, etc.) will be employed in the agricultural sector, and only 10 per cent (45 million people) will migrate to the cities. The remaining 180 million workers, 40 per cent of the total, will be employed in the rural non-agricultural enterprises (RMRB, 19 March 1984; Xu and Ye, 1985; Li QZ, 1986a; Li QZ 1986b).

If these projections come true, there would, at that time, be about 1.35 cultivators for one hectare (assuming a total cultivated surface kept at 100 million hectares). In 1983, such a density was in fact achieved by a farming couple in the Wuxi region (Jiangsu): they seemed to achieve the right land/labour ratio as the number of work days then effectively used for one hectare of wheat crop was no more than seventy-one, about the same as the requirements we estimated previously (Li *et al.*, 1985). Without any major change in agricultural technology and especially without further mechanization of agricultural tasks, then full employment could be reached in Chinese agriculture by the year 2000.

However, in order to reach such a target, about 100 million new jobs will have to be created in rural non-agricultural enterprises, in addition to their present level of 75 million workers (120 million new jobs in the more likely assumption of 465 million people as rural manpower) – and only 50 million peasants would have then migrated to the cities.

The Chinese authorities believe that it will thus be possible to restrain the rural exodus at a very low level, while the rise of rural industries will continue in the growing number of small towns. This official belief is supported by quite a number of Chinese economists who put forward the following (and sometimes stereotyped) arguments.

The first one, ritually invoked, is that the Chinese way is a specific one, which cannot automatically follow the Western examples of large city urban development and great industrial concentration, blamed for having been built on the ruins of the rural economy (Yuan BJ, 1985).

Then, instead of a massive rural exodus drawing the best elements of the countryside out of the villages, they favour a progressive urbanization built on the development of small towns, in symbiosis with the surrounding villages. In this scheme, an agricultural exodus would take the place of the rural exodus, the peasants 'leaving the fields without leaving the countryside, entering the workshops without migrating to the cities' (*litu bu lixiang, jinchang bu jincheng*; Wang XM, 1985).

The rural industrialization, which would be the very basis of such an urban development, would then escape the heavy investments of urban infrastructures; it would stimulate the utilization of local resources and in particular the on-the-spot transformation of agricultural products. With capital investment thresholds much lower than those of the great industry, the rural enterprises could more easily absorb local manpower surpluses; more flexible employment structures would also preserve the links of the workers with their former villages. On the other hand, land concentrations could be achieved in a countryside free from its excess manpower, and economies of scale would then facilitate the specialization and the modernization of agricultural production, while the villages would also participate in the benefits of market-towns' economic growth, mainly through the remittances and salaries of non-agricultural workers (Liu and Guo, 1985).

Taking argument from the present unbalanced structure of the cities, which favours the very great ones, the supporters of the development of small towns consider that such a development can achieve a more balanced, pyramidal structure, with great cities on top of a large base of small towns. These would constitute a stratified urban network covering all the countryside, with, at the bottom, the township seats with small shops and basic services for the peasants (there are now 90,000 townships for one million administrative villages), followed by market-towns grouping industrial enterprises at the junction points of communications and exchanges (these market towns could number up to 10,000), and on the top, the county seats providing centres for administrative, cultural and economic activities (there are about 2,000 counties at present (Zhang YL, 1985).[5] That would leave about 300 cities of over 100,000 inhabitants where the concentrated, 'city-type' part of the urban population is concerned.

They stress that just a doubling of the present market-town population would absorb almost 200 million people out of the 480 million urban persons that China is supposed to comprise in the year 2000 (on an assumed total population of 1.2 billion persons, the rate of urbanization then reaching 40 per cent). These 200 million more people would correspond precisely to those 100 million new workers that, as we know, should find a job in the rural enterprises (Zhen *et al.*, 1985).

Other Chinese economists consider that all the preceding arguments and calculations are just a brilliant exercise in wishful thinking. They underline all the limitations constraining the development of small rural industries. The fragmentation of their markets, the local character of their resources, the small scale of their operations are prohibitive in view of the necessary concentrations which are at the very basis of the industrialization process. Their primitive technology makes these rural industries less competitive than the urban ones when they try to enlarge their markets and enter in competition with the large industry of the cities. They like to point out that rural enterprises do well only when they work on a sub-contracting basis with the big factories of the cities: so rural industry would only prosper in the shadow of very large towns (Ke BS, 1985).

According to the same economists, small towns do not constitute an ideal environment for industrialization. The construction of new infrastructures in the countryside would be much more expensive than the mere development of existing ones in the big cities. The dispersion of workshops and housing would aggravate the loss of arable land, already diminishing due to the industrial and urban expropriations. The pollution, itself, would be more severe and less manageable with a multitude of small enterprises using archaic technologies and difficult to control effectively. Finally, the lack of efficient service networks and the cultural backwardness of the surrounding countryside would be a formidable handicap, discouraging the rise of a true modern economy (Wu TQ, 1985).

Very logically, these economists propose an accelerated industrialization through the development of big cities. According to them, one cannot escape the historical law of the parallel development of both industries and cities. Only big towns, and not the market towns of the countryside, can realize the labour concentration, market density, the economies of scale in infrastructure and proximity of services necessary for industrial processes of production (Ke BS, 1985).

They then criticize the present policy controlling the development of big cities and pushing only the growth of small towns. Some scholars expose the past policy of constraining any rural exodus as an unjustified protection of urban privileges, such as (relatively) high salaries, social benefits for housing, education, health, numerous subsidies, etc., which could only prosper under the shelter of Malthusian practices for workers' employment. They bluntly propose to open these urban strongholds to the peasants, with reservations in the use of some quotas according to local situations (Song GQ, 1985). Others go even as far as recommending the abolition of any control on population migration in order to give way to free play of economic forces alone in the search of an optimal urban growth (Chen S, 1986; Guo and Xia, 1986).

Lastly, other economists – one of them none other than the well-known sociologist Fei Xiaotong – harbour more intermediate views. They support the development of small towns in a first stage of *agricultural* exodus, but they do not deny that a second stage will be necessary afterwards, implying then a true *rural* exodus. They also point out the great necessity of developing medium cities (100,000 to 500,000 inhabitants) as well as small towns: these medium cities are the missing link between the great towns and the countryside, particularly evident in the inner provinces of China (Cai L, 1985; Fei XT, 1985).

The questionable rise of rural enterprises

At least all these arguments are proof of the openness of debate in China today (some people even do not hesitate to propose the abolition of the 'hukou' system, which is the very basis of police controls in the present Chinese political regime). It is not proposed to decide which is right and which is wrong among all these professed opinions. An attempt will be made simply to try to use available statistics and investigations in order to throw light on different aspects of the debate.

The recent rise of Chinese rural enterprises, the so-called 'enterprises of townships and market towns' (*xiangzhen qiye*), seem to lend weight to the supporters of an urbanization process based on the development of rural industry. The figures are really impressive: in 1980, there were 25 million people employed by these enterprises which generated a gross value of 60 billion yuans (agricultural enterprises excluded); in 1986, there were 75 million people for 330 billion yuans (current prices), implying an average annual growth of 20 per cent for manpower and 33 per cent for the gross value of production (RMRB, 4 June 1987)[6] In the brief lapse of time of six years, about 50 million new jobs therefore have been created by these rural enterprises and the official objective of 100 million new jobs to be created by the year 2000 does not seem out of reach.

However, a closer examination of these figures leads to some reservations, even if it does not invalidate the reality of an extraordinary progess. The 1980 and 1985 figures are not quite comparable. Until 1983, the only registered enterprises were the collective ones, belonging to the communes (townships) and brigades (villages). After 1983, statisticians began to add enterprises owned by individuals or by private peasants' associations. Indeed, most of these family (or groups of families) enterprises have been created since 1984, but in any case it cannot be excluded that the early 1980 figures underestimate by a certain margin the whole volume of non-agricultural activities, as they exclude the small cottage industries and family shops. So, the progress has been less rapid than suggested by the official statistics, a fraction of the newly 'created' jobs being only the registration of previously omitted activities. If we consider only the collective enterprises of townships and villages, the average annual growth rate between 1980 and 1985 is much lower than the preceding figure: about 10 per cent for manpower, and 25 per cent for the gross value of production.

In fact, the main part of the last three years' growth was precisely constituted by the very fast rise of family enterprises. In 1985, their labour force amounted to more than 40 per cent of rural non-agricultural workers in China (Table 2.11). They spread principally in the commerce, services and transportation sectors, making up more than 80 per cent of employees. In the process, they have achieved a more balanced structure for rural non-agricultural employment. In 1980, industrial activities employed three-quarters of the workers of collective enterprises, while today they only employ half. So, the tertiary sector could make up for its past slow development. However, it is still quite underdeveloped compared to other Asian countries where trade and services employ up two thirds of rural non-agricultural manpower (Ho, 1986: 38). Thus, it can be hoped that a further progress in this sector's employment will be observed. But one may wonder whether it will be so possible to create the millions of jobs that have to be found by the year 2000.

As for the transportation sector, it seems that some kind of saturation has already been reached. It is a physical saturation as some 430,000 trucks, 850,000 tractors and 4.6 million hand-tractors (which are used mainly for the transport of goods, and are 84 per cent privately owned) are congesting the rural roads, which were not designed for such a traffic and are now almost completely clogged (TJNJ, 1986: 148; Xinhua Agency, 23 June 1986). Without massive investments for the upgrading of the rural road network, long neglected in the past, it will be very difficult to increase by a big margin the number of jobs already existing in this kind of trade.

There remain the rural industries proper, which are still the main component for rural non-agricultural jobs and constitute the driving force, best able to induce employment in the other sectors, and are therefore the favourite hope for supporters of small town development.

These industries have become an important part of the national economy (Table 2.12). Their workers are more than one third of all those in Chinese factories, more than one half in the construction sector. The gross value of their production is one-fifth of that of Chinese industry as a whole and one-third for construction. Their portion of national production is 26 per cent of coal, 25 per cent of textiles, 24 per cent of paper, 21 per cent of sugar, 20 per cent of cement, etc. (JJYJ, 1986, 8: 9–24). Within the rural sector in 1985, the rural non-agricultural enterprises employed 18 per cent of the total rural manpower, generated 43 per cent of the gross value of all rural products and services, with industry and construction as the main part (12 per cent of rural manpower and 36 per cent of the gross value of productions and services in rural areas).

These figures are really impressive, particularly when we consider the fast growth of recent years (the gross value of township and village enterprise production increased by 46 per cent for industry and 48 per cent for construction in 1985 compared to the 1984 level) (TJNJ, 1986: 215). But these figures, too, may be a little misleading. Part of the growth, in terms of the gross value of production, can be considered as somewhat artificial, especially for the spectacular rises observed after 1984. This gross value is inflated by the growing amount of raw materials wasted by less and less efficient workshops, as well as by the inflation of the prices of such materials often purchased at a high price on the free market, outside the channels of allocated goods ruled by State planification. At least, these were the conclusions of an investigation carried out in the rural industries of Jiangdu, Jiangsu province. There, the gross value of production doubled in 1985, compared to 1984, but the profit was reduced by half as the cost of raw materials and energy (70 per cent of the total cost price) soared, the stocks piled up and the capital rotation slowed down (Xue and Zhao, 1985). At the national level the same trend can be observed with the figures covering all the collective enterprises of townships and villages (mostly industrial or transportation ones): their gross value of production tripled from 1980 to 1985, but their net profits went down from 18 per cent of gross value to less than 9 per cent (Table 2.10).

To be sure, the recent rise of small rural industries is real enough, as is the creation of almost 25 million new jobs between 1980 and 1985 in the factories and the construction sector (Table 2.11). But their future growth remains questionable. In recent conferences a great number of Chinese economists have questioned the overheated growth of recent years, as they wondered whether rates of increase as high as 60 per cent observed in Jiangsu province in 1985, were symptomatic of healthy development or, on the contrary, were the manifestations of an uncontrollable growth, both hollow and dangerous for the balanced economy of whole regions.[7] In particular, it seems more and more difficult to go on financing such a fast-growing expansion. The prevalent lax credit policy for rural enterprises has been accused (Yan and Han, 1986). It is a fact that rural enterprises are absorbing a growing portion of available financial resources: between 1982 and 1985 net loans to these enterprises tripled, with more than 35 billion yuans in 1985 representing 45 per cent of the total agricultural loans granted by the Agricultural Bank and Rural Credit Co-operatives (NYNJ, 1986: 327; Ma YW, 1987). In 1983, in

Shifang county, Sichuan province, rural enterprises already used two-thirds of budgeted aid to agriculture and more than one third of agricultural loans; a prospective study then showed that the projected growth of these enterprises for the three following years would need capital funds double of what local resources could afford (Zhou and Han 1985; Zhou YB, 1985).[8] At a national level, detailed studies are lacking, but the problem is certainly quite similar. And therefore, for this reason alone, it is clear that the rate of increase of small industrial enterprises will not be maintained at its present high level.

However, the rural industries have a lot of strong points. At least at the beginning, the small rural workshops benefit from real comparative vantages against the large State factories, particularly as concerns capital investment thresholds for every new job created and the productivity of fixed assets. An investigation, carried out in 1980 in the Jiangsu province on the industrial enterprises of brigades and communes, resulted in the following demonstrative ratios: the fixed assets per employed worker were only 928 yuans in the small enterprises compared to more than 10,000 yuans in State industry, the value of production for every 100 yuans of fixed investment was respectively 339 yuans (small enterprises) and 188 yuans (State enterprises), with respective profits of 14.8 yuans and 11.4 yuans. Economies of scale showed up only for the value of output per employed worker: 3,448 yuans in rural enterprises against 15,755 in the State ones (Zhen *et al.*, 1985).

These figures clearly show the greater capacity of small rural enterprises for absorbing labour, as well as their better productivity of invested capital. So the supporters of rural industrialization should be right in their beliefs. However, one must note that these industries in China seem to be losing their edge as time passes: during 1980–85, the fixed assets per employed worker in the collective enterprises on townships and villages have grown from 1,088 yuans (comparable to 928 yuans observed in Jiangsu) to 1,807 yuans in 1985. The corresponding increase in the productivity of invested capital (from 2.01 to 2.65) is not convincing as we saw that part of it may be considered as void (see above and Table 2.10).

The relevance of the average figures of comparative advantages for rural small-scale industries may be also questioned. It has been demonstrated in other countries that fixed asset thresholds, productivity of capital as well as of labour, varied considerably from one branch to another within rural industries, according to the size of the workshops, the technology employed, etc. (Little, 1987). The detailed distribution by branches or by types of factories is not available for the whole of rural China. Anyway, we can observe great variations across labour size and the value of production in the distribution by branches of townships and village industries presented in Table 2.13. Township factories have an average size double that of village workshops (56 workers against 24), the scales of enterprises (excluding cottage industries) vary from six workers for village food industries to 135 for township textile factories.

Moreover, this table shows very clearly that these enterprises, although located in the countryside, do not work much for the processing of agricultural products. The two outstanding industries, both by their proportion of manpower and value of production, are mechanics and building materials: these two industries total up to nearly one half of the labour force and the value of production.

The food industry is particularly narrow based with only 8 per cent of the workers and of the production. Yet, this is a branch where comparative advantages are quite obvious: fixed assets per worker are only 3,500 yuans, compared to 7,960 in State factories. Nevertheless, this kind of rural enterprise achieves only 10 per cent of the total food business in China – a food business which remains itself quite underdeveloped (JJYJ, 1986, 8: 18). Even where particular efforts were made, as in the area of Wujiang (Jiangsu province), to develop integrated chains of production ('agro-industrial-commercial' ones, *maogongnong*) such as aquaculture, rabbits (fur and pelts), poultry (eggs and feathers), etc., the value of such products still did not reach a quarter of total rural enterprise production (Guo LS *et al.*, 1985).

On the whole, if we include textile industries which are doing well in the countryside, the processing (in a large sense) of agricultural products concerns only one-third of rural enterprises. We are then very far away from the situation of an industrial development mainly based on agriculture. The agro-industry branch seems to be, on the contrary, the weak link in rural enterprises. An investigation, conducted in the Suzhou area (Jiangsu province), has indicated that, in 1984, the agro-industry enterprises generated only 32 per cent of the total value of rural industry. In this locality, well-known for its mulberries and silk production, the silk factories are paradoxically backward and the silk products quite primitive (70 per cent of the silk fabrics produced for export are made up of raw silk with low competitivity on world markets because of their poor quality) (Zhou *et al.*, 1985). There are plenty of examples of this kind in the numerous investigation reports available. It would seem that the agro-industry is particularly handicapped by primitive technologies, high prices of raw materials, and, on top of this, by heavy taxes imposed by the State which reaps substantial profits from them (Liu and Song, 1985).

Conversely, the most active branches of rural industries are those which use local raw materials (not necessarily agricultural) and work in co-operation with large urban companies. The most convincing example may be found in Shazhou, another locality of Jiangsu province, where the rural industry is indeed quite prosperous: it represents 80 per cent of the total industrial production of the county, about four times the value of local agricultural production. It is mainly based on small metallurgy, chemicals, mechanics, construction as well as textiles. The workshops of Tangqiao (a township of this same county) produce fabrics using synthetic fibres as well as the local wool from the surrounding countryside. They also produce concrete, glass-wool, etc. using local materials, but their produce is marketed in Shanghai, no more than 100 kilometres away. Moreover, almost 60 per cent of this township's enterprises are linked by subcontracting agreements with the big factories of the Shanghai metropolis (CZ, 1985, 12: 4–7).

This example of Shazhou leads us to one of the main problems raised by the Chinese economists during their controversy: the rural industrialization process seems particularly strong precisely in well-developed areas, benefiting from dense communications networks, and where most of the big cities of China are located. The spatial distribution of rural industries speaks for itself (Table 2.14). We can see that the coastal provinces of China, from Liaoning to Guangdong, the more advanced ones with 60 per cent of the national industrial production for less than 40 per cent of total population, group the major part of rural industries: 51 per cent of their manpower, 64 per cent of their production. These are the very provinces where most of the big cities of China can be found (Peking, Tientsin, Shanghai, Canton), and they dispose of the best roads and of any waterways (totalling 56 per cent of total Chinese road and water freight). Still more conclusive, the eastern part of these coasts, composed of the two highly urbanized provinces of Jiangsu and Zhejiang, around the Shanghai conurbation, covers 19 per cent of the manpower of rural industries and 28 per cent of production value for only 11 per cent of China's total inhabitants.

So, is rural industry only growing fast in the shadow of cities and big towns, as stated by those criticizing priority for the small towns?

Of course, such a statement is too abrupt to be true. But one cannot help being struck by the contrast between such an advanced county as Shazhou, located in one of the most developed coastal areas of China, with booming rural industries, and, on the other hand, backward counties of the inner provinces, such as Mianyang in Sichuan province. Mianyang, in the rich red basin of Sichuan, is not under-privileged as such, but, as with most of these mainly agricultural regions of China which it portrays very adequately, this county was quite under-urbanized in 1982: 90 per cent of the population were still peasants, and underemployed peasants too, as one-third of them were officially counted as surplus labour, while commune and brigade industries employed only 5 per cent of the total rural manpower. Shazhou on the contrary employs more than half of its labour force in the rural workshops, most of them grouped in 23 big market-towns, served by close communication networks, with a great number of services. The difference is not only in economic resources or infrastructures, it stems also from the respective levels of education of the populations. In Mianyang, the 1982 census numbered up to 37 per cent illiterate (or semi-literate) persons of over twelve years, and less than 5 per cent of them graduated from high school (Li HR *et al.*, 1985). In Shazhou 22 per cent of workers in rural enterprises had graduated from the local high schools, and 44 per cent from the secondary schools.

Then we cannot escape the question of the very possibility of the future development of rural industry in the inner regions, which constitute the major part of China, and where the expansion of non-agricultural jobs is the more necessary as agricultural underemployment is much more severe there than in the developed coastal areas (Deng YM, 1985). Of course this question cannot be answered easily. But the whole future of the Chinese way of industrialization and urbanization axed on rural enterprises and small towns' development will depend on this answer.

Two models and their implications

Somewhat paradoxically, Chinese economists have not researched appropriate models for such a rural industrialization in those regions of inner China which are most concerned. They have found them in those eastern coastal areas where small township and village enterprises are already well-developed. The two provinces of Jiangsu and Zhejiang, around Shanghai, have been intensively investigated (Fei XT, 1984; 1986), and each of them has supplied its own model: the Wenzhou model for Zhejiang; the Suzhou model for Jiangsu. These two embody quite appropriately the two contrasting ways now offered to China: the way of an aggressive rural capitalism, and the socialist way of a collective, or at best self-managed, economy.

The Wenzhou municipality, located at the back of a bay in the south of Zhejiang province, had long been an overpopulated region. With 6.2 million inhabitants for 193,000 cultivated hectares, the population density was as high as 32 persons per cultivated hectare and underemployment was rampant everywhere in the countryside in which 1.6 million agricultural workers constituted 89 per cent of rural manpower in 1978.

In that rather backward context, the rise of small enterprises has been noticeably fast, particularly in the six coastal counties of the municipality. In 1985, agricultural workers numbered only 600,000 persons, about 29 per cent of the total rural workforce, against 1.3 million workers and employees in the secondary and tertiary sectors. The agricultural over-population was then somewhat deflated with no more than 3.1 workers per cultivated hectare in 1985, compared to 8.3 seven years earlier.

This extraordinary change, transforming a mainly agricultural

From: *Cataloging*
To: Binding Unit
Date: _10-19-90_
Initial: _MKW_

Call no.: HX
550
A37
C65
1990

Torn page(s)_____

Tip in loose
  page(s)_____ ✓

Mend spine_____

Loose score_____

Pam bind_____

Single issue_____

Make portfolio_____

Forward_____

Make a pocket_____
Other:

From: Binding Unit
4-6872; Ex. 47

Done: _____

Initial: _RD_

Date: _10/25/90_
(if different
from sender's)

Need to bind
  by commercial
  binder:_____

Suggest withdraw:___

Other:

Form #: 1982-April-28
          1982-May-6

municipality into a busy industrial centre within a few years, was achieved through the spontaneous development of family enterprises, which now include half of the non-agricultural workers. Moreover, they generate two-thirds of the gross value of production of this new rural industry (1.07 billion yuans out of a total of 1.66 billion). This rural industry, which covered only 17 per cent of the value of the rural production in 1978, has now risen to 65 per cent of this value (Zhang GS *et al.*, 1986).

The small workshops, employing an average of 2.5 persons each, have therefore succeeded in absorbing no less than 1 million workers within a few years, if we count all the service activities they induced. This is about two-thirds of previous agricultural manpower! What, then, was the secret behind such an astounding performance?

This secret seems to lie in a thorough specialization of family industry production, coupled with an efficient commercialization network concentrated in a few markets of national importance.

Entire market-towns have specialized in the production of simple consumer goods for daily life, using local raw materials or scraps from big industry. In this way, they produce millions of buttons, badges, plastic flowers, baskets, number-plates, plastic shoes, small electrical appliances, ready-made clothes, etc. The specialization has induced an upgrading of equipment and products (zip fasteners following on from button production, men's suits after children's shirts, etc.). Different family workshops also specialize in successive stages of production.

Such a scattered industrial production could not go far without an efficient network of tradesmen, who lend the necessary materials and funds to the families, and take charge of the marketing of finished products, functioning therefore in a classical putting-out system. More than 100,000 merchants or tradesmen go all over the countryside signing contracts. They then supply 415 markets, of which 120 specialized ones, to which thousands of buyers come from all over China, previously contacted by the very mobile dealers of Wenzhou. Ten of these markets have acquired national fame, such as the button market of Qiaotou, which provides the whole of China with this very simple, but so basic product of first necessity (a very complete range of 1,300 different types of buttons is available in Qiaotou). There is also the Liushi market for electric appliances, etc.

This commercial network is completely beyond State control. The merchants have formed their own associations for the services they needed, such as private companies supplying trade information, private transport companies (able to guarantee delivery of goods anywhere in China, within twenty days!), etc. These enterprises' financing is totally independent too. The budgeted State aids and the loans from the Agricultural Bank and Credit Co-operatives amount to less than 15 per cent of the circulating funds used by this industry (Cheng SL, 1987).

The quasi-totality of the 780 million yuans fixed assets of the rural workshops has been self-financed or provided by numerous tontines (or mutual rotating credit societies, with traditional modes of organization, such as the *juhui*, the *yaohui*, etc.) which are tapping local private savings (Li RX, 1986).[9]

Thus, these industrial or commercial enterprises are representative of a true small rural capitalism, even if there are only a few dozen 'great families', realizing hundreds of thousands, even millions of yuans in turn-over. There is a true financial market, and a labour market too (every day, in the market town of Jinxiang, dozens of young girls come down from the neighbouring mountains in search of jobs). Its dynamism is at the root of this newly built and prosperous rural industry in the very place where past commune and village collective enterprises were almost non-existent. It has also generated a vigorous urbanization process, with sixty towns newly settled in the past three years (they now number eighty-four in total) that were built with the founding of local government resources, multiplied by growing fiscal revenues and also with the funding of private investment (600 million yuans have been invested in new urban settlements since 1983). May such an example be reproduced in other parts of China?

The Wenzhou region is very special indeed. From long ago it was well-known for its old family craft traditions as well as for the great abilities of its tradesmen. As an overpopulated area it has been for a long time an old centre for emigration, and its overseas communities had long ago already reproduced this Wenzhou model of cottage industry (it is precisely the case of the cloth industry in Paris, in its major part reorganized along such family workshops run by Wenzhou immigrants settled in the Sentier district). Its supporters in China believe, anyway, that such a model can be exported to other places on the Chinese continent. They admire its great flexibility and, above all, stress that it costs nothing to the State, a forceful argument in times of financial difficulties.

The Wenzhou model's vantage point, besides the inherent dynamism of any capitalist development, is to specialize precisely in the loopholes left by the State planification (buttons for example), thus complementing State industries rather than competing with them. In that respect, it differs noticeably from ordinary rural industries, accused by many Chinese economists of merely duplicating branches of big industry without true specialization on possible strong points (JJYJ, 1986, 8: 20 sq).

Indeed, the other localities of China which have followed the Wenzhou model have also specialized in previously neglected production in which they occupy a dominant position on the Chinese market: for example, about 120 villages of Qinghe county (Hebei province) produce 60 per cent of the national demand for motocycles spare parts; the same district supplies one third of all cutlery in China (Zhang *et al.*, 1987).

So, local possibilities exist here and there, particularly in a region where old craft traditions exist. But even then, official permission for such activities is still necessary. In Li Xian (Hebei province), traditional production of wool fabrics as well as of leather products was only revived after public rehabilitation by the authorites of more than one hundred old cadres, formerly condemned for having encouraged such capitalist activities. These official authorizations, which must proceed from political will, are more necessary because private small scale enterprises need some public shelter in order to survive in a bureaucratic environment. They must use some officially tolerated tricks such as paying big State enterprises to make money transfers for them (access to bank accounts is not easy for individuals in China) or even pay their taxes; they must pull the strings of established 'connections' (*guanxi*) within the administration in order to get necessary transport documents in time, etc. (Zhang GS *et al.*, 1986).

Indeed, many cadres in China do not at all appreciate the competition with this kind of dynamical capitalism. And there are Chinese economists too, who oppose the Wenzhou model and support instead the Suzhou model, still called the 'model of south Jiangsu' (*Sunan moshi*).

Suzhou is a locality well-known for its beautiful scenery. It is located along the 'Great Canal' and belongs, as does the major part of this southern part of Jiangsu province, to the hinterland of the Shanghai metropolis. Less overpopulated than Wenzhou (5.4 million people, of whom 3.6 million peasants, on 368,000 hectares, make a density of 'only' fifteen persons per cultivated hectare, of whom ten living on agriculture), the Suzhou region has benefited from an earlier industrialization, and in 1980 almost 600,000 workers and employees already worked in local rural enterprises, that is to say, one-quarter of total manpower.

In 1985, there were 1.1 million people working in these enterprises, up to 41 per cent of the 2.7 million rural workers of the whole region. The peasants then, have lost one-quarter of their labour force within five years. Less spectacular than in Wenzhou, the rise of rural industries here was none the less quite sustained, following a trend that began long ago. As a matter of fact, the province of Jiangsu, where Suzhou stands, had already started its rural industrialization process, with high rates of growth during the previous fifteen years: these annual rates of growth, for the gross value of production, were 26 per cent from 1970 to 1975, 36 per cent from 1975 to 1980, 27 per cent from 1980 to 1985 (with two peak years in 1984 and 1985). In 1985, this ancient industrialization trend made Jiangsu the top province as far as the rate of non-agricultural employment in the rural manpower is concerned: about 30 per cent against an average 18 per cent for the whole of China.

In Suzhou, as well as in the rest of South Jiangsu, this sustained development was due mainly to collective enterprises of townships and villages. Family non-agricultural activities occupy just a minor position with only 3 per cent of the gross value of production. Such a dominance of big collective workshops, each of them with an average of 82 workers, is matched by the superiority of industry on other trades: the mills produce 70 per cent of the 9.6 billion yuans, gross value of the total rural non-agricultural enterprises' production (the non-agricultural activities alone represent 69 per cent of the gross value of Suzhou's rural activities) (Meng XD *et al.*, 1986).

The great scale of Suzhou region's enterprises is also shown in a higher ratio of fixed assets per worker than in Wenzhou (2,150 yuans against about 1,000 yuans) as the technologies used in mechanics, metallurgy, chemicals, textiles, etc. are much more elaborate. On the whole, the ratio of the gross value of production (9.63 billion yuans) to fixed assets (2.36 billion yuans) is as high as 4:1 for the average of all enterprises.

Most of these enterprises, and this is a special feature of the Suzhou model, have concluded sub-contracting agreements with city firms, in this case Shanghai of course. In Changzhou (which belongs to the administrative region of Suzhou), no less than two-thirds of rural workshops are linked in this way to the great companies of Shanghai, with which they form what the Chinese call 'bands of enterprises' (*qiye qunti*), grouping in an integrated chain of production both the small workshops of the countryside and the big factories of the city. For example, the cloth industry, which employs 5,000 workers in 92 enterprises of Changzhou, is integrated into the operations of two general mills in Shanghai, sub-contracting 370,000 pieces of clothing each month. This kind of integration puts rural production back into the juridiction of the State plan, while upgrading and standardizing the quality of its products. For example, Wujin sewing-machines increased its production tenfold, and its profits 25 times after being integrated by the general sewing-machine company of Changzhou (Jin XY, 1986). Quite plainly, the advantage of this Suzhou model has much to do with the proximity of the Shanghai metropolis, therefore its proper relevance is somewhat affected.

Its supporters stress the point that these collective rural enterprises are in the best position to reinvest part of their profits back into agriculture. Private companies of Wenzhou cannot claim such utility as they only gave back 6 yuans for each cultivated hectare as aid to agriculture in 1985 (Cheng SL, 1987). Suzhou collective enterprises, for their part, contributed a total of 450 million yuans to agriculture from 1979 to 1985, about 245 yuans annually per cultivated hectare (Pan *et al.*, 1985). These rural enterprises thus forcefully contributed to the uninterrupted increase of peasant revenues, from 157 yuans per person in 1978 to 706 yuans in 1985 (38 per cent of the latter coming from rural industries).

The high level of such contributions to peasants (about 30 per cent of enterprise profits) reflect the fact that the management of these collective undertakings is not free, but subject to the strict control of local authorities. The counterpart of their utility for agricultural progress is the clumsiness of official management, resulting in the financial weaknesses that everybody acknowledges. In Suzhou, at the beginning of 1986, 30 per cent of rural collective enterprises were in the red, the average profit rate of the whole industry fell by half (Meng XD *et al.*, 1986; Xue JJ, 1986).

This problem is not specific only to Suzhou. In fact, most of the Chinese collective township and village enterprises reveal the same shortcomings in their management, resulting from the confusion of administrative and economic powers. At township level, in most cases, administrative cadres are also the bosses of the enterprises belonging to their juridiction. The cadres are tempted by, and most often succumb to, the lure of multiplying the enterprises' activities in order to inflate their turnover and at the same time increase local government revenues through additional taxes (*tanpai*) on this same turnover, or through retention (*tiliu*) of part of the profits. These questionable methods are put to good use such as funding road repairs, electrification of the countryside, maintenance of schools, etc. They are also used for the construction of luxury municipal buildings, for buying office cars for the cadres, etc. (Cao GY, 1986; Chen QY, 1986).

It would seem, as a rule, that taxes take about half the gross profit of enterprises in South Jiangsu (in contrast with Wenzhou where half the enterprises escape taxation). Of the remaining net profit, local authorities still withhold half for aid to agriculture, for infrastructure works, etc. (Cheng SL, 1987). The result of such practices is a startling drop in the self-financing capacity of the collective enterprises which must rely heavily on public loans for their expansion. Self-financing contributed to no more than one-third of total investments of these enterprises in Jiangsu in 1985 (Gu SN, 1986).

At a national level, in 1984, only 2 billion yuans were reinvested for enlarged reproduction out of a total of 12.8 billion yuans net profits earned by the collective enterprises of townships and villages. That same year, public loans to these enterprises increased by some 15 billion yuans (Zhou CQ, 1986).

So the quality of the management of such enterprises certainly has something to do with the financial difficulties which mar their future development (Zhou CQ, 1986). This questionable management is in fact related to the ambiguous state of ownership, particularly at township level: whether these collective enterprises are the property of the township governments which are their real bosses; the property of an ideal collective of the workers (agricultural ones or not) of the whole township; or the property of the restricted body of their sole employees.

Beyond the controversies of theoreticians, it seems that township level collective enterprises are very similar to State ones, except for their size and their market orientation. The very reform recipes that are being tried on their management system – proportional sharing of their profits, payment to the authorities of a fixed amount deducted from the profits, complete responsibility for losses or profits after tax payment – are just the same as those formerly tried on State enterprises (Pan *et al.*, 1987). Some people suggest freeing these enterprises from administrative interference by granting them true self-management status: distribution of fixed assets to the employees, enlargement of capital by the issuing of shares, democratic designation of managers by the share-holders' assembly only, etc. (Cao GY, 1986).

Of course, such proposals are vigorously opposed by the lobbies of township cadres. As in Wuhu (Anhui province), they put forward the fact that the past development of these enterprises has been their own doing, and that it could not continue without their help (Yu SD, 1986). It is quite true that the past years' rapid rise of rural industry corresponds to the massive reconversion of local cadres who threw themselves into business as there was no more work for them within a now decollectivized agriculture (Oi, 1986).

Even if these collective enterprises are assumed to be regulated by the market for 80 per cent of their activities (He and Li, 1985), their close links with local administrations make them more of an extension, however special such an extension may be, of socialist economics than a potential basis for autonomous rural capitalism.

Thus there exists a true dilemma for Chinese authorities: will they encourage the pursuit of the Wenzhou model, a capitalist one, with its own dynamism but unable to develop the agricultural hinterland, or will they favour the Suzhou model, a socialist one, theoretically more able to aid agriculture but hampered by clumsy management and numerous financial problems? This last model benefits from the early start acquired by old communal industries, but the former one is now catching up. On the one hand, many village collective enterprises are contracted to individual managers and harbour quasi-private features. On the other hand, cottage industries, still in a minority position, are growing at a fast pace. For example, in the Pearl River delta, where collective workshops still hold 90 per cent of the value of production, the family enterprises are developing rapidly and already employ one-quarter of the whole non-agricultural manpower: in Nanhai county, their rate of growth is three times that of collective work shops for which they become quite dangerous competitors (Lu YJ, 1986).

The encircling of the cities by waves of rural capitalist enterprises is still just an image quite far from reality, but one cannot exclude that it may come true at some point in the future.

Appendix 2.1 Towards an adequate numerical picture of urbanization

In Chinese terms, the 'urban population' is composed, on one hand, of the inhabitants of the 'cities' (*shi*), most of them counting more than 50,000 persons, and, on the other hand, of those of the small 'towns' (*zhen*), with 2,000–3,000 people, most of them non-agricultural. The Chinese definition of 'urban' people varied mostly as to the inclusion, or not, of the 'agricultural' component of the inhabitants of the cities, and also as to the minimal size and 'non-agricultural' composition of the small towns considered as urban ones.

According to the geographers Chan and Xu, the official data, from 1952 to 1985 in the statistical yearbook, consist of the 'total urban population' (*shizhen zongrenkou*), therefore including 'agricultural' people of the near suburbs of great cities, as well as those of the small towns. As far as 1982, at least, the official data could then be considered as adequately describing the real degree of urbanization in China. For these two specialists, the distinction between 'agricultural' and 'non-agricultural' inhabitants of the cities is not an operational one for the definition of the true 'urban' dimension of the population, as this definition only concerns the rules of distribution of rationed grain in the cities (Chan and Xu, 1985).

According to the city planning specialist, Kirby, this same set of data does not include the 'agricultural' population of the cities before 1964. (However, for this early period, agricultural people of the small towns were partially or totally included in the official count.) He considers that only the 'non-agricultural' population of the cities is meaningful for the measure of urbanization, arguing that some large cities have annexed in their suburbs big tracts of agricultural land, the peasants then being counted as 'urban' people having no real town-dwellers' qualities (Kirby, 1985: 54–102). He so proposes another set of 'urban population' (*chengzhen renkou*), more restrictively defined, excluding the 'agricultural' component of the cities, meaning then a lower rate of urbanization in China (Table 2.1, 2nd column of Urban Population).

The Chinese sources we had access to confirm Kirby's interpretation: before 1964, the official set of figures excludes the agricultural population of the cities, but comprises the whole population, non-agricultural as well as agricultural, of the small towns (Wei JS, 1985). This is very clear from the censuses of 1953, 1964 and 1982 which give us the repartition of the population by size of cities and towns, those of 1953 and 1982 distinguishing precisely total urban population and 'non-agricultural' urban population (Tables 2.2 and 2.3). So, it is manifest that the official set of data is not consistent, and that the figures of the pre-1964 period cannot be compared with those of the following years.

Another difficulty comes from the number of 'urban' market-towns, which declined from one census to another: they were 5,404 in 1953, 3,148 in 1964 and only 2,664 in 1982 (on the other hand, the number of cities increased from 166 in 1953 to 244 in 1982). It seems that in 1953, the norms defined in 1955 were still not applied (these norms specified that the urban towns must have a minimal population of 1,000 to 2,000 people, more than 75 per cent of whom being non-agricultural, or a population of more than 2,000 people, at least 50 per cent non-agricultural). Then, in 1953, about 1,700 administrative small towns were abusively counted as urban, inflating the total population of cities and towns by more than four million people. In 1964, on the contrary, the 1955 norms were reinforced, urban towns' criteria being upgraded to the minimum size of 2,500–3,000 inhabitants (more than 85 per cent non-agricultural) or over 3,000 inhabitants (more than 70 per cent non-agricultural). In 1982, the same norms as 1964 were used again, but about 377 county seats were excluded from the count, being considered as too agricultural (Zheng ZH, 1983; Kirby, 1985: 73–85). So, the decrease of the number of towns from 1953 to 1982 corresponds to stricter norms for the definition of 'urban' dwellings. It means, too, that during all this period, the development of small towns stagnated altogether. But we will come back to that question later.

For the years 1952, 1957, 1960, 1964, 1976, 1982 and 1985, we have tried to establish consistent sets of figures, both for 'total urban population' and for the 'non-agricultural urban'. Of course, we have taken into account all the changes in definitions; we also took note of the fact that available official figures for the non-agricultural urban population, after 1964, exclude the agricultural component of the small towns (see Table 2.1, columns Total Urban Population, and Non-Agricultural Urban Population). For the figures of non-agricultural urban population from 1952 to 1982, we used Kirby's data only, removing 12 million people from the pre-1964 figures in order to exclude the agricultural inhabitants of the small towns, and four million people more for the pre-1955 figures, thus excluding the very small towns abusively counted as urban in the 1953 census. These corrections are, without doubt, quite rough. Anyway, the few data on the non-agricultural urban population published by the Chinese demographers basically confirm our estimations (for example, Zhou Yixing, in Zhou YX, 1984, quotes non-agricultural rates of 13.1 per cent for 1957 and 16.6 per cent for 1960, our estimates being respectively 13.3 and 18 per cent.

The contrast between the two sets of urban population we so established is quite amazing. The evolutions of the two sets are parallel up to 1982, but the difference between the two levels of urbanization they imply is enormous. For the total urban population, we verify that, after the rapid growth of the 1950s and the short-lived peak of 1960, the urbanization remained stagnant at about 17–18 per cent of the total population during most of the 1960s and 1970s. It increased again to 21 per cent as recently as 1982. Measured through the 'non-agricultural' urban population, this degree of urbanization is considerably lower, with 14 per cent to 12 per cent only of the total population from 1964 to 1976. It reaches no more than 15 per cent in 1982.

After 1982, the two sets diverge totally. The total urban population is rapidly inflating up to 37 per cent of the total inhabitants of China in 1985. On the other hand, the 'non-agricultural' urban population, which is increasing too, but at a much lower pace, still constituted only 18 per cent of the total Chinese population at the same time, half as much as the preceding figure. The spectacular difference between these two assessments of the urban population stems mainly from the evolution of the small towns. After the decline of their number which was as low as 2,700 in 1982 (or 3,050 including all county seats), they abruptly went up to as high as 7,500 in 1985 (*China Daily*, 8 December 1986). At that same time, the 'agricultural' component of their inhabitants, which was less than 25 per cent in the 1982 census, was growing up to 60 per cent, according to our estimates (Tables 2.2 and 2.3).

Can we reasonably consider that the population of this crowd of new market-towns, or agglomerations of big villages, may be counted as true urban dwellers? The published results of Chinese surveys give us some reasons to question such an assumption. For example, Yiyang region, of Hunan province, in 1978, counted five small towns (county seats), with 40,000 inhabitants each, 14 market towns, with 13,000 inhabitants each (87 per cent of them non-agricultural), against 209 commune headquarters (2,500 persons each) and 3,350 villages (1,000 persons each): so, the urban population numbered less than 400,000 persons for a total population 4.3 million people, less than 10 per cent, mirroring quite well the situation in most of comparable agricultural regions of China. In 1985, there were still the same five small towns, with 40,000 persons each, and the 3,350 villages, but the number of 'urban' market-towns had been tripled: they were then 42, with the same 13,000 inhabitants each but only 41 per cent were then non-agricultural. Certainly, the total urban population then reached 750,000 persons, 16 per cent or the total population of 4.6 million people in 1985, but the 'non-agricultural' component had not changed noticeably still with about 400,000 persons. A detailed analysis of the population of all these new 'urban' market-town settlers showed that they were constituted, in their major part, by former peasants, with their home and families still in the original villages belonging to the newly established towns, commuting every day to the market-centre where they worked (Xie and Shi, 1985).

For the whole of China, the inhabitants of such market-towns have grown from 61 million persons in 1982 (30 per cent of the total urban population) to more than 170 million in 1985 (45 per cent, almost half of the total urban population!) (Table 2.2). Most of them may be considered as mixed workers, both employed by workshops and in the fields (*yigong, yinong*), their links with their original villages still preserved, and not as true city dwellers. If the increase of the number of 'urban' market towns means a real change of activities in the rural areas, we are of the opinion that its impact on the level or urbanization in China is better measured by counting only the 'non-agricultural' component of these towns (even if the distinction between 'agricultural' inhabitant/'non-agricultural' one – having the right to buy rationed, subsidized, food grain – is not always meaningful.

In the same manner, by counting only the 'non-agricultural' part of the population of the cities, we eliminate all the cases of artificial 'very great towns' with only 10 per cent to 50 per cent of non-agricultural inhabitants. These cases are often found in mine areas: Xintai, in Shandong province, had 1.16 million inhabitants in 1985 but only 170,000 non-agricultural ones, Puyang, in Henan province, 130,000 non-agricultural ones in a total population of 1.09 million persons, etc. On the whole, of the 57 cities of more than 1 million persons in China (total urban population), 21 had a majority of agricultural inhabitants at the end of 1985 (see the list in *Xinhua Agency*, 26 June 1986).

Appendix 2.2 Statistical tables

Table 2.1: Urbanization rates 1952–85

	Total population	Urban population (1) Official million	%	(2) Kirby million	%	Total urban population million	%	Non-agricultural urban population million	%
1952	574.8	71.6	**12.5**	71.6	**12.5**	80*	**13.9**	56*	9.7
53	588.0	78.3	13.3	78.3	13.3				
54	602.7	82.5	13.7	82.5	13.7				
55	614.7	82.9	13.5	82.9	13.5				
56	628.3	91.9	14.6	91.9	14.6				
1957	646.5	99.5	**15.4**	99.5	**15.4**	112*	**17.3**	88*	**13.6**
58	659.9	107.2	16.2	107.2	16.2				
59	672.1	123.7	18.4	123.7	18.4				
1960	662.1	130.7	**19.7**	130.7	**19.7**	164	**24.8**	119*	18.0
61	658.6	127.1	19.3	127.1	19.3				
62	673.0	116.6	17.3	116.6	17.3				
63	691.7	116.5	16.8	116.5	16.8				
1964	705.0	129.5	**18.4**	99.2	**14.1**	130	**18.4**	99	**14.0**
65	725.4	130.5	18.0	101.7	14.0				
66	745.4	133.1	17.9	102.7	13.8				
67	763.7	135.5	17.7	103.5	13.6				
68	785.3	138.4	17.6	104.5	13.3				
69	806.7	141.2	17.5	105.5	13.1				
70	829.9	144.2	17.4	106.5	12.8				
71	852.3	147.1	17.3	107.5	12.6				
72	871.8	149.4	17.1	108.3	12.4				
73	892.1	153.5	17.2	109.6	12.3				
74	908.6	156.0	17.2	110.5	12.2				
75	924.2	160.3	17.3	111.7	12.1				
1976	937.2	163.4	**17.4**	112.4	**12.0**	163	**14.4**	112	**12.0**
77	949.7	166.7	17.6	116.2	12.2				
78	962.6	172.5	17.9	122.8	12.8				
79	975.4	185.0	19.0	133.6	13.7				
80	987.1	191.4	19.4	140.3	14.2				
81	1,000.7	201.7	20.2	146.6	14.6				
1982	1,015.4	211.5	**20.8**	152.9	**15.1**	212	**20.8**	153	**15.1**
83	1,025.0	241.3	23.5						
84	1,034.8	330.1	31.9						
1985	1,045.3	382.4	**36.6**			382	**36.6**	186*	**17.8**

Sources: TJNJ 1986: 91; Kirby 1985: 107, 114, 121; Wei, JS in RKYJJ, 1985, 6: 29.
Explanation of terms:
All percentages refer to the first column, that is, the total population of China (Taiwan excluded).
Urban population (1) = official number; (2) = as estimated by Kirby, op. cit.
Total urban population includes the 'agricultural' population of suburbs and small towns.
* Author's own estimations or interpolations.

Table 2.2 Repartition of total urban population 1953, 1964, 1982, 1985

Urban settlements by size (inhabitants) categories	1953			1964			1982			1985		
	Number	Population million	%	Number	Population million	%	Number	Population million	%	Number	Population million	%
All cities and towns	5568	86.2	100	3316	130.4	100	2908	206.3	100	7800	382.44	100
of which towns	5402	33.71	39	3148	40.0	31	2664	61.06	30	7500	170.57	45
Cities only	166	52.49	61	168	90.39	69	244	145.25	70	324	211.87	55
Total population	–	582.6	100	–	694.6	100	–	1008.2	100	–	1045.3	100
% in cities	–	–	9	–	–	13	–	–	14.4	–	–	20.3
% in cities and towns	–	–	14.8	–	–	18.8	–	–	20.5	–	–	36.6
Cities by size categories (inhabitants in million and as % of all cities, excl. towns)												
> 2.0	4	13.97	27	7	25.80	29	13	43.76	30	13	46.20	22
1.0 – 1.99	5	7.05	13	9	12.97	14	25	31.62	22	44	54.84	26
0.5 – 0.99	16	11.29	21	34	25.10	28	47	33.21	23	85	60.61	29
0.3 – 0.49	10	3.96	8	30	11.96	13	48	18.52	13	78	30.40	14
0.1 – 0.29	68	11.95	23	69	13.19	15	89	16.74	11	93	19.29	9
< 0.1	63	4.27	8	19	1.37	1	22	1.40	1	11	0.53	<1

Sources: For 1985 from TJNJ 1986: 94; for the other years from Wei, JS in RKYJI, 1985, no. 6: 35.

Notes: The population figures for 1953, 1964, and 1982 are mid-year numbers, the percentages of the total population of cities and towns slightly differ from those presented in Table 1 for the same years, which are based on end-year numbers.

Table 2.3 Repartition of non-agricultural urban population 1953, 1982, 1985

In urban settlements by size (inhabitants) categories	1953 Population (non-agric.)			1982 Population (non-agric.)			1985 Population (non-agric.)		
	number	million	%	Number	million	%	Number	million	%
All cities and towns	5568	77.3	100	2908	143	100	7800*	186*	100
of which towns	5404*	33.73†	44†	2669*	46	32	7500*	68*	37
Cities only	164	45.53	56	239	97.12	68	324	118.26	63
Total population	–	582.6	100	–	1008.2	100	–	1045.3	100
% in cities	–	–	7.5	–	–	9.6	–	–	11.3
% in cities and towns	–	–	13.3	–	–	14.2	–	–	17.8
Cities by size categories (non-agricultural) (inhabitants in million and as % of all cities, excl. towns)									
> 2.0	⎰ 9	11.61*	27*	7	25.20	26	8	29.30	25
1.0 – 1.99	⎱	5.86*	13*	13	16.85	17	14	18.17	15
0.5 – 0.99	16	9.38	22	28	19.93	21	30	21.92	19
0.3 – 0.49	⎰ 77	3.25*	7*	31	11.94	12	45	16.96	14
0.1 – 0.29	⎱	9.80*	23*	105	19.55	20	150	26.78	23
< 0.1	62	3.63	8	55	3.65	4	77	5.13	4

Sources: For 1983 Kirby 1985: 150; for 1982 TJNJ 1986: 107 and Kirby 1985: 150; for 1985 TJNJ 1986: 94.
Notes: For 1953 mid-year numbers, for 1982 and 1985 end-year numbers. – Total town population of 1953 includes its agricultural share.
* Interpolated figures
†Excluding the agricultural share, the population in 1953 was 64 million for cities and towns, with 20 million in towns only, accounting for a share of 31 instead of 44 per cent in total non-agricultural urban population (this total population of cities and towns accounting then for 11 instead of 13.3 per cent in the total population of China).

Table 2.4 Repartition of the population of cities of more than 100 000 inhabitants, 1953, 1964, 1982, 1985

City sizes (by million inhabitants)	Total urban population				Non-agricultural urban population		
	1953	1964	1982	1985	1953	1982	1985
> 2.0	29	29	30	22	29	27	26
1.0 – 1.99	15	15	22	26	15	18	16
0.5 – 0.99	23	28	23	29	23	21	19
0.3 – 0.49	8	13	13	14	8	13	15
0.1 – 0.29	25	15	12	9	25	21	24

Sources: See Tables 2 and 3 and also their nomenclature.

Table 2.5 Rural-urban migrations, 1952–85 (millions of persons)

	Population change total (annual average)	of which: natural increase	migration (derived) total/annual average
1952–1957			
Total China	575 → 647 = + 72 (= + 2.4% p.a.)	not applicable	not applicable
Non-agric. urban	56 → 88 = + 32 (= + 9.5% p.a.)	+ 13	+ 19 = + 3.8 p.a.
Rural	519 → 559 = + 40 (= + 1.5% p.a.)	+ 59	– 19 = – 3.8 p.a.
1957/1960			
Total China	647 → 662 = + 15 (= + 0.8% p.a.)	(of which a 10 million decrease in 1960)	
Non-agric. urban	88 → 119 = + 31 (= + 10.6% p.a.)	+ 6	+ 25 = + 8.3 p.a.
Rural	559 → 543 = – 16 (= – 1 % p.a.)	+ 9	– 25 = – 8.3 p.a.
1960–1964			
Total China	662 → 705 = + 43 (= + 1.6% p.a.)	(of which a 4 million decrease in 1991)	
Non-agric. urban	119 → 99 = – 20 (= – 4.5% p.a.)	+ 12	– 32 = – 8 p.a.
Rural	543 → 606 = + 63 (= + 2.8% p.a.)	+ 31	+ 32 = + 8 p.a.
1964–1976			
Total China	705 → 937 = + 232 (= + 2.4% p.a.)	not applicable	
Non-agric. urban	99 → 112 = + 13 (= + 1 % p.a.)	+ 18	– 5 (+ 1 p.a.)*
Rural	606 → 825 = + 219 (= + 2.6% p.a.)	+ 214	+ 5*
1976–1982			
Total China	937 → 1015 = + 78 (= + 1.3% p.a.)	not applicable	
Non-agric. urban	112 → 153 = + 41 (= + 5.3% p.a.)	+ 8	+ 33 (+ 2.7 p.a.)*
Rural	825 → 862 = + 37 (= + 0.7% p.a.)	+ 70	– 33*
1982–1985			
Total China	1015 → 1045 = + 30 (= + 1 % p.a.)	not applicable	
Non-agric. urban	153 → 186 = + 33 (= + 6.7% p.a.)	+ 4	+ 29 = + 9.7 p.a.
Rural	862 → 859 = – 3 (= – 0.1% p.a.)	+ 26	– 29 = – 9.7 p.a.

Sources: TJNJ 1986: 91; Kirby 1985: 107, 114, 121; author's estimates.

Notes:

* The migration balances for these years are gravely distorted by 17 million urban youngsters, who were sent to the countryside during 1964–76 ('Cultural Revolution') and returned to the cities during 1976–82. In the table, their numbers form part of the overall results of migration for each of the two periods, but not of the annual averages, which show only the 'normal' migration rate and therefore are put in parentheses.

Table 2.6: Total, rural, and agricultural labour numbers, 1952–85

	Total labour in China	Rural/county population	Rural labour millions	% RP	% TL	Agric. labour (official) numbers	Rural enterp. labour	EHA lab	Estimated number of agric. labour millions	% RL	% TL
1952	207	520	182	35	88	173	7*	2*	173	95	84
1957	238	560	206	37	87	193	11*	2*	193	94	81
1960	230x	540*	182*	34	79	170	10*	2*	170	93	74
1965	287	624/591	235	40	82	234	2*	3*	230	98	80
1976	388	825/787	301	38	78	291*	18*	4*	279	93	72
1977	394	833/797	303	38	77	291*	20*	4*	279	92	71
1978	399	840/803	303	38	76	291*	23	4*	276	91	69
1979	406	842/807	306	38	75	291	24	4*	278	91	68
1980	419	847/811	314	39	75	298	25	4*	285	91	68
1981	433	854/819	322	39	74	307	26	4*	292	91	67
1982	447	862/828	333	40	74	312	28	4*	301	90	67
1983	460	/835	343	41	75	317	29	5	309	90	67
1984	476	/843	354	42	74	317	49	5	300	85	63
1985	499	859/844	371	44	74	304	67	6	298	80	60

Sources: TJNJ 986: 124; TJNJ 1983: 122; TJNJ 1983: 122; 147, 206; NYNJ 1981: 9; NYNJ 1982: 16; NYNJ 1983: 19, NYNJ 1985: 120; NYNJ 1986: 152–154.

Notes:

Unit million persons; RP – Rural Population; RL – Rural Labour; TL – Total Labour.

NB   Rural/county population – rural (i.e. total less non-agricultural urban) and county population (i.e. people of communes, or townships, and villages); Rural labour collective and individual rural man power (% RP – as % of rural population; % TL – as % of total Chinese labour); Rural enterp. labour – non agricultural labour force of rural enterprises; EHA Lab. – Employees of Education, Health and Administration sectors; Estimated number of agric. labour % RL – as % of Rural Labour, % TL – as % of total Chinese labour. * Author's estimates or interpolations

Table 2.7 Indices (1952=100) of agricultural labour productivity, 1957–85

Year	Agricult. revenue* 1	Agric. labor (official) number 2	Agric. revenue per agr. worker (official) 1/2	Gross agr. prod.† 3	Agric. labor (author's estimate) 4	GAP/per estim. agric. worker 3/4	Grain production Total ‡ 5	Grain production per estim. worker 5/4
1957	120.1	111.6	107.6	124.8	111.6	111.8	118.7	106.4
1960	83.6	98.3	85.0	96.4	98.3	98.1	86.7	88.2
1965	122.9	135.3	90.8	135.7	132.9	102.1	121.0	91.0
1976	168.4	168.2	100.1	188.3	161.3	116.7	178.2	110.5
77	166.6	168.2	99.0	187.4	161.3	116.2	175.9	109.0
78	174.6	168.2	103.8	202.7	159.5	127.1	196.4	123.1
1979	187.2	168.2	111.3	218.2	160.7	135.8	206.7	128.6
80	188.3	172.3	109.3	229.0	164.7	139.0	199.5	121.1
81	202.4	177.5	114.0	243.9	168.8	144.5	202.2	119.8
1982	225.9	180.3	125.3	271.2	174.0	155.9	220.6	126.8
83	247.6	183.2	135.2	292.5	178.6	163.8	241.0	134.9
84	283.5	183.2	154.7	328.2	173.4	189.3	253.5	146.2
1985	301.6	184.4*	163.6	339.5	172.3	197.0	235.9	136.9

Sources: TJNJ 1986: 44, 53, 167, 180, and preceding Table 2.6.
Notes:
* Including village industries
† Excluding village industries
‡ Adjusted for 1952, 1957, 1960
All indices are in comparable terms.
Agricultural revenue includes that of village industries.
Gross agricultural production (Gross agr. prod., GAP) is in value terms and excludes village industries.
Grain production is adjusted for 1952, 1957, 1960.

Table 2.8 Sources of peasant families' revenues (Hubei)

Revenues	1954 yuan	1954 %	1964 yuan	1964 %	1974 yuan	1974 %	1979 yuan	1979 %	1982 yuan	1982 %	1984 yuan	1984 %
Total per person of which:	83.5	100	118	100	106.2	100	161.8	100	286.1	100	392.3	100
agriculture	71.0	85	105.0	89	100.1	94	147.8	91	231.9	81	300.4	77
Crafts	4.3	5	1.4	1	0.9	1	0.9	1	2.3	1	–	–
Construction and transport	1.3	2	0.5		–	–	} 1.6	1	18.1	6	–	–
Trade, restaurants and	} 0.3	–	} 0.8	1	–	–	}		1.9	1	–	–
services									1.9	1		
Ind. and other	6.6	8	10.3	9	5.2	5	11.5	7	24.0	8	–	–
Total non-agricultural	12.5	15	13.0	11	6.1	6	14.0	9	54.2	19	91.9	23
(of which labour rev.)	(6.7)	(8)	(5.4)	(5)	(4)	(4)	(7.3)	(5)	(33.5)	(12)	(55.7)	(14)

Sources: 1954 to 1982, Samuel HO 1986: 37; 1984, *Hubei Tongji Nianjian* 1986: 365.
Note: Ind. and other – Industrial salaries and other non-agricultural revenues.

Table 2.9 Commercialization rates of agricultural products, 1952–85

	Agr. procurements % of ag. production	Free market % of ag. procurement	Gross grain procurements % of grain in output	Resales % grain procured
1952	**42.7**	**8.4**	**20.3**	**15.0**
1957	**43.2**	**6.1**	**24.6**	**29.5**
1965	**44.3**	**4.2**	**25.0**	**31.0**
1976	**39.2**	**4.7**	**20.3**	**30.1**
1977	41.7	4.4	20.0	33.7
1978	41.7	5.6	20.3	30.8
1979	**40.4**	**6.7**	**21.7**	**28.2**
1980	43.8	8.2	22.8	34.3
1981	47.5	9.4	24.2	37.9
1982	47.5	10.2	25.9	35.7
1983	48.5	10.5	30.9	28.9
1984	49.0	11.8	34.8	33.2
1985	**51.3**	**16.8**	**30.5**	**49.6**

Source: TJNJ 1986: 167, 539, 542, 624.
Notes: Agr. procurements % of ag. production – Value of agricultural procurements, in percentage of gross value of agricultural production (forestry, secondary productions and rural industries excluded); Free market % of ag. procurements – Part of free market in total agricultural procurements; Gross grain procurements % of grain output – Volume of gross grain Procurements in percentage of grain output; Resales % grain procurements – Part of resales to Peasants in total grains procurements.

Table 2.10 Evolution of rural enterprises 1978–85

	1978	1979	1980	1981	1982	1983	1974	1985
Township and village enterprises								
Number (thsd) enterprises	1,524	1480	1425	1337	1362	1346	1650	1569
Manpower (million workers)	28.3	29.1	30.0	29.7	31.1	32.3	38.5	41.5
Gross value of product. (billion yuan)	49.1	54.3	65.7	72.9	85.3	101.7	143.3	198.8
Taxes (% gross of value of prod)	4.5%	4.2%	3.9%	4.7%	5.2%	5.8%	5.5%	5.5
Net profits (% of gross value of prod.)	18.0%	19.2%	18.1%	15.5%	13.5%	11.6%	9.0%	8.5
Fixed assets (billion yuan)	23.0	28.0	32.6	37.4	42.9	47.6	57.5	75.8
Turnover capital (billion yuan)	9.5	13.3	17.7	20.1	23.1	26.3	39.9	59.5
Labour numb./per enterprise (persons)	18.5	19.7	21.1	22.2	22.9	24.0	23.3	26.6
Gross. value of prod./per worker (yuan)	1,736	1868	2189	2454	2740	3143	3724	4780
Fixed assets/per worker (yuan)	812	963	1088	1258	1379	1471	1494	1800
Gross value of prod./per value of fixed assets	2.13	1.94	2.01	1.95	1.99	2.14	2.49	2.65
Individual or associated enterprises								
Number (thsd) of enterprises							4415	10655
Manpower (million workers)							13.6	28.3
Gross value of prod. (billion yuan)							27.7	74.5
Taxes (% of gross value of prod.)							4.2	3.8
Net profits (% of gross value of prod.)							21.2	15.6
Labour numb/per enterprise (person)							3.1	2.7
Gross value of prod./per worker (yuan)							2035	2634
Total of rural enterprises								
Labour numbers (million persons)							52.1	69.8
Gross value (billion yuan)							171	273.3

Source: NYNJ 1986: 324 (NB: the enterprises include a small number with activities registered as 'agricultural').

Table 2.11 Labour numbers of rural enterprises in 1980, 1982, 1985

	Industry million	%	Transport million	%	Construction million	%	Trade & services million	%	Total million	%
1980 Commune									13.9*	
" Brigade									11.5*	
" Total	19.4	76	1.1	4	3.4	13	1.5	6	25.4	100
1982 Commune									15*	
" Brigade									12.7*	
" Total	20.7	75	1.2	4	4.2	15	1.6	6	27.7	100
1985 Township	13.3		} 1.2		} 7.9		} 2.1		21.1*	
" Village	14.5								17.9*	
" Indiv. & Ass.	7.6*		7.8*		3.4		9.5*		28.3	
" Total	35.4*	53	9*	13	11.3	16	11.6*	17	67.3	100

Sources: 1980, TJNJ 1981: 193; 1982, TJNJ 1983: 206.
1985, TJNJ 1986: 215, 220, 505, NYNJ 1986: 160–161.
Note: Indiv. & Ass. – Individuals & associations.
* Author's estimates

Table 2.12 Rural enterprises in national economy, 1985

	Gross value of production				Labor numbers			
	Rural/sector 10^9 *yuans*	*%*	*National* 10^9 *yuans*	*Rur/Nat* *%*	*Rural/sector* 10^6 *persons*	*%*	*National* 10^6 *persons*	*Rur/Nat.* *%*
Total rural of which	634	100	1.631	39	371	100	499	74
agriculture	362	57			298	80		
Non-agric. enterprises	272	*43*			67	*18*		
Industry	175	28	972	18	35x	9	91*	38
Construction	51	8	163	31	11	3	21	52
Transport	19	3	44	43	9x	3	17*	53
Trade & Services	27	4	90	30	12x	"	34*	35

	Production in physical units		
	Rural sector	*National*	*Rur/Nat* *%*
Electric energy (10^9 KwH)	7.6	410.7	2
Coal (10^6 t.)	228	872	26
Mach.-tools (un.)	6,300	167,200	4
Cement (10^6t.)	29	146	20
Pesticides (10^3 t)	59	211	28
Paper Carton (10^6 t)	2.2	9.1	24
Salt (10^6 t)	1.3	14.8	9
Sugar (10^6 t)	0.95	4.51	21
Vegetable oils (10^6 t)	1.19	4.01	30

Sources: TJNJ 1986: 36, 124, 215, 299–302 and Table 11.
Notes: *Rural Sector* – Cooperative and private only. *Rur/Nat* – Rural as a percentage of national enterprises.
* Author's estimates
Units million persons; billion yuans; million or thousand tons; billion KwH

Table 2.13 Repartition by branches of township and village industries, 1985

	Labour		Gross. Val. Prod		Labor number per enterprise		Gross val. prod. per worker	
	million workers	%	billion yuan	%	Towns	Villages	Towns yuan	Village yuan
Metallurgy	0.704	2.5	4.9	3.4	82.2	37.3	7,615	6,190
Electricity	0.132	0.5	0.5	0.3	12.2	3.4	4,205	2,993
Coal	1.545	5.6	5.6	3.8	92.1	46.9	3,616	3,667
Petroleum	0.015	–	0.2	0.1	22.5	25.0	13,649	10.800
Chemicals	1.779	6.4	12.3	8.4	56.6	36.6	8,565	5,565
Mechanics	4.817	17.3	37.3	25.6	54.0	33.9	8,605	6,765
Constr. Mat.	8.303	29.8	27.6	18.9	77.2	31.1	3,549	3,126
Wood	0.969	3.5	4.3	2.9	27.1	16.5	4,930	4,005
Food	2.167	7.8	11.5	7.9	22.4	6.4	6,847	4,242
Textiles	2.129	7.7	18.2	12.5	134.5	58.7	9,478	7,201
Cloth	1.303	4.7	5.4	3.7	63.1	41.8	4,497	3,705
Leather	0.482	1.7	2.3	1.6	66.1	51.3	5,242	4,473
Paper	0.577	2.1	3.5	2.4	60.5	42.7	7,139	5,220
Books & Cult	1.258	4.5	4.4	3.0	67.9	42.6	3,845	3,243
Others	1.637	5.9	7.9	5.5	33.8	21.4	5,638	4,543
Total	27.817	100	145.9	100	55.6	23.6	6,015	4,544
					Average	32.6	Average	5,246

Source: TJNJ 1986: 220.
Note: Gross val. product.: Gross value of production

Table 2.14 Spatial repartition of rural enterprises, 1985

	Total Population		Gross Value Indus. Prod.		Vol. transport road + water		Labor in rural enterprises		Gross Rev. of Rur. Enterpr.	
	million	%	billion yuan	%	billion ton/km	%	million	%	billion yuan	%
Coastal Prov.	391.2	38	553.4	60	57.9	56	35.8	51	16.0	64
(of which East)	(114.6)	(11)	(245.4)	(27)	(30.9)	(30)	(13.5)	(19)	(7.6)	(28)
Inner Prov.	356.8	34	212.6	23	31.7	31	22.3	32	6.0	24
Rear Prov.	293.1	28	159.6	17	13.9	13	11.7	17	31.6	12
Total China	1041.0	100	925.6	100	103.5	100	69.8	100	256.6	100

Sources: NYNJ 1986: 160, 226; TJNJ 1986:93, 282, 389.

Notes: Percentages are in terms of Chinese totals.
  Coastal Provinces: Liaoning, Beijing, Tianjin, Hebei, Shandong, Jiangsu, Shanghai, Zhejiang, Fujian, Guangdong.
  Of which = East: Jiangsu, Shanghia, Zhejiang.
  Inner Provinces: Jilin, Shanxi, Henan, Anhui, Hubei, Hunan, Jiangxi, Guangxi.
  Rear Provinces: Heilongjiang, Inner Mongolia, Shaanxi, Qinghai, Ningxia, Gansu, Xinjiang, Guizhou, Yunnan, Sichuan, Tibet.

Notes

1. For the uncertainties of the agricultural reforms see Aubert, 1986b.
2. The term 'involution' was first proposed, in a quite different context, by Clifford Geertz (1963). We are using it here in a more restrictive sense.
3. According to Tang Tianhua and Zhou Jiaxiang (1987), material expenses per kg of grain have increased by 45 per cent from 1978 to 1985.
4. The 'townships', or xiang, correspond to the former People's Communes (communes' seats and villages).
5. This concept is likely to have been influenced by the works of W. Christaller (1893-1969) (personal communication of K.E. Wädekin).
6. The general inflation in China which affects the prices of products and services of these enterprises explains partly such a high rate of growth.
7. These conferences have been referred to in numerous Chinese articles. See, for example, Xue JJ, 1986; *compte-rendu* of a conference of December 1985 in NYJJWT, 1986, 4: 17–21; detailed arguments of another conference in NYJJWT, 1986, 5: 50–2; see also Gu SN, 1986.
8. Zhou Chengquiong (Zhou CQ, 1986) quotes an investigation made in nine provinces where capital needs for new enterprises would be four times the local financial resources available.
9. The Chinese authorities begin now to acknowledge the existence of private mutual credit societies, and many investigations have been published. See, for example, Mei LD (1985) on private credits in the countryside, and Chen, Z. (1986) on traditional credit organizations.

References

Sources in Occidental languages

Aubert, C. (1981) 'Temps de travaux agricoles et sous-emploi dans les campagnes chinoises', *Rapport d'Enquête en Chine Rurale*, Paris, INRA: 14sq.
Aubert, C. (1982) 'Chine rurale: la révolution silencieuse', in *Projet*, September-October: 955–71.
Aubert, C. (1984) 'La nouvelle politique économique dans les campagnes chinoises', in *Le Courrier des Pays de l'Est*, July-August: 3–32.
Aubert, C. (1985) 'Chine: le décollage alimentaire?' in *Études Rurales*, July-December: 25–71.
Aubert, C. (1986a) 'La baisse des récoltes de grains en 1985, un échec ou une transition?', in *Aujourd'hui la Chine*, June: 11–13.
Aubert, C. (1986b) 'Les réformes agricoles, ou la genèse incertaine d'une nouvelle voie chinoise', in *Revue Tiers-Monde*, October-December: 727–54 (special issue 'Les Réformes en Chine').
Banister, J. and Woodard, K. (1987) 'A tale of new cities, rapid urbanization is changing the contours of the China market', in *The China Business Review*, March-April: 12–21.
Buck, J.L. (1937) *Land Utilization in China*, University of Nanking: 302.

Chan, K.W. and Xu, X., (1985) 'Urban population growth and urbanization in China since 1949: reconstructing a baseline', in *The China Quarterly*, December: 583–613.

Geertz, C. (1963) *Agricultural Involution, the processes of ecological change in Indonesia*, University of California Press, Berkeley.

Hauser, P.M. and Gardiner, R.W. (1980) *Urbanization Urban Growth and Intermediate Cities, trends and prospects*, Honolulu, cited in Armstrong and McGee, 'Les Villes du Tiers-Monde', in *Revue Tiers-Monde*, October-December 1985: 830.

Ho, S.P.S. (1986) *The Asian Experience in Rural Nonagricultural Development and its Relevance for China*, The World Bank, Washington: 4–7.

Kirby, R.J.R. (1985) *Urbanization in China: Town and Country in a Developing Country, 1949–2000 AD*, New York, Columbia University Press.

Little, I.M.D. (1987) 'Small manufacturing enterprises in developing countries' in *The World Bank Review*, **1**, 2: 203–35.

NCNA, (1985) *New China News Agency*, 15 December (quoted in *BBC Survey of World Broadcasts*, Far East W 1370).

Oi, J.C. (1986) 'Commercializing China's rural cadres', in *Problems of Communism*, September-October: 1–15.

Sources in Chinese language

Abbreviations for periodicals

CMJJ	*Caimao Jingji* (Finance and Trade Economics)
CZ	*Caizheng* (Finances)
JGLLYSX	*Jiage Lilun Yu Shixian* (Theory and Practice of Prices)
JJDL	*Jingji Dili* (Economic Geography)
JJYJ	*Jingji Yanjiu* (Economic Researches)
NCJR	*Nongcun Jinrong* (Rural Finance)
NMRB	*Nongmin Ribao* (Peasants' Daily)
NYJJWT	*Nongye Jingji Wenti* (Problems of Agricultural Economics)
NYJSJJ	*Nongye Jishu Jingji* (Economy of Agricultural Technology)
RKYJ	*Renkou Yanjiu* (Demographic Researches)
RKYJJ	*Renkou Yu Jingji* (Demography and Economy)
RMRB	*Renmin Ribao* (People's Daily)
ZGNCJJ	*Zhongguo Nongcun Jingji* (Rural Economy of China)
ZGSHKX	*Zhongguo Shehui Kexue* (Social Sciences in China)

Abbreviations for Yearbooks

NYNJ	*Zhongguo Nongye Nianjian* (China's Agricultural Yearbook)
TJNJ	*Zhongguo Tongji Nianjian* (China's Statistical Yearbook)

Articles and books

Cai L (1985) in NYJJWT, July: 4–8.

Cao GY (1986) in NYJJWT, December: 18–21.
Chen QY (1986) in NYJJWT, June: 40–2.
Chen S. (1986) in NYJJWT, October: 12–15.
Chen Z. (1986) in NYJJWT, December: 28–31.
Cheng SL (1987) in NYJJWT, January: 17–20.
Deng YM (1985) in NYJJWT, December: 23–7.
Fei XT (ed.) (1984) *Xiao Chengzhen, Da Wenti* (Small Towns Big Problem) Jiangsu Press.
Fei XT (1985) in NYJJWT, March: 3–5.
Fei XT (ed.) (1986) *Xiao Chengzhen, Xin Kaituo* (Small Towns, New Developments), 1986.
Gu SN (1986) in NYJJWT, May: 15–17.
Guo LS *et al.* (1985) in NYJSJJ, May: 39–42.
Guo ST and Xia KR (1986) in ZGNCJJ, December: 22
He JW and Li XG in NYJSJJ, November: 13–15.
Jin XY (1986) in NYJJWT, March: 30–2.
Ke BS (1985) in NYJJWT, February: 59–62.
Li HR *et al* (1985) in NYJJWT, July: 12–15.
Li JK, Shen LQ and Chen GY, in NYJSJJ, May: 20–4.
Li QZ (1986a) in NYJJWT, October: 8–11.
Li QZ (1986b) in ZGNCJJ, December: 18–21.
Li RX (1986) in NYJJWT, April: 8–12.
Li YZ (1986) *Unpublished report on grain costs of production in China*, Beijing, Agricultural Economics Institute, Chinese Academy of Agricultural Sciences, July: 12–14.
Liu FC and Guo WG (1985) in RKYJ, June: 17–18.
Liu GY and Song PQ, in NYJSJJ, June: 30–2.
Liu ZP (1987) in NYJSJJ, January: 22–4.
Lu YJ (1986) in NMRB, 20 October.
Ma YW (1987) in NCJR, March: 5.
Mei LD (1985) in CMJJ, August: 51–3.
Meng XD *et al* (1986) in NMRB, 16 October.
NYSC (1984) *Nongye Jishu Jingji Shouce* (Agricultural Technical Economy Handbook), Beijing, Agricultural Editions, rev. ed.: 642–4.
Pan S, Zhou YZ and Zhu HM (1985) in NYJJWT, August: 17–19.
Pan S, Zhou YZ and Zhu HM, in ZGNCJR, March: 23–7.
Shen LR (1985) in NYJJWT, February: 19–22.
Song GQ (1985) in NYJJWT, July: 9–11.
Tang TH and Zhou JX (1987) in JGLLYSX, January: 17
Wang XM (1985) in JJYJ, February: 16–21.
Wei JS (1985) in RKYJ, June: 28–35.
Wu TQ (1985) in NYJJWT, March: 49–51.
Xie C and Shi XY (1985) in RKYJ, June: 36–8.
Xinhua Agency, 26 June 1986: quoted in *BBC, Survey of World Broadcasts*, Far East W 1396.
Xu TX and Ye ZC (1985) in RKYJ, May: 16–20.
Xue F and Zhao CZ (1985) in NYJSJJ, September: 38–40.
Xue JJ (1986) in NYJJWT, April:. 4–7.

Yan JS and Han C (1986) in NYJJWT, March: 26–9.

Yu SD (1986) in NYJJWT, December: 23.

Yuan BJ (1985) in NYJJWT, October: 41–5.

ZGMYWJ (1984) *Zhongguo Maoyi Wujia Tongji Ziliao, 1952–1983* (Statistical Materials on Prices and Trade in China, 1952–1983), Beijing Statistical Editions: 21.

Zhang GS *et al* (1986) in NMRB 11 October.

Zhang GS, Wang CB and Wang ZM (1987) in NMRB, 18 February.

Zhang YL (1985) in JJYJ, January: 12–18.

Zhen WM, Ye KL and Chen G, in NYJJWT, April: 43–6.

Zheng ZH (1983) in ZGSHKX, April: 119–36.

Zhou CQ (1986) in NYJJWT May: 22–4.

Zhou Pand Han ZC (1985) in NCJR, May: 25–8.

Zhou YB (1985) in NYJJWT, March: 44–6.

Zhou YX (1984) in JJDL, February: 119.

Zou HF, Wang GX, Zhao FB, in NYJSJJ, October: 23–5.

Chapter three

Socialist agriculture outside Europe: new ways in Mongolian agriculture?

Guenter Jaehne

Questions and parameters of the presentation

Looking at 'new developments' in the agriculture of the Mongolian People's Republic (MPR), one has to deal with past developments, that is, in retrospect, and with the likely future, that is, with prospective developments. Considering the past, the question comes to mind, whether ideas of a specific Mongolian way towards a socialized agriculture developed in the MPR, and if so, whether they basically differed from the notion of a 'collectivized economy' as put into practice in the USSR and Eastern Europe.

As to the prospective, one would have to investigate present developments with a view to the foreseeable future, such as: What further developments of the Mongolian agriculture may reasonably be expected? Are there any policy changes or efforts discernible or are reforms of the agricultural planning and administration system imminent, which may lead the country out of its critical food situation? It does not seem impossible, for example, that Ulan Bator will refer to recent developments of Chinese agriculture.

Also, a definition of the term 'new development' is required in order to avoid its being used too loosely. Concerning production in general, it is easy to enumerate quite a number of new developments. Without doubt, crop production – especially of grain, potatoes and fodder – was greatly improved and enlarged in comparison with the very minor role this branch played before collectivization. In addition, the increased pork and chicken production has to be mentioned, which in earlier times was a domain of the Russian and Chinese settlers in the country, whereas Mongolians avoided these animals. Among other new developments is the expansion of irrigation.

Such subjects, although legitimate in themselves, will not be dealt with in the present paper. After some general information on the country and a chronological overview of the collectivization process, it focuses on the socio-economics and policy of agriculture and deals with four aspects:

1. a short retrospective summary providing a background for the present situation;
2. a description of the actual critical situation in the domestic supply of food, especially of meat;
3. an overview of the plans conceived by the leaders of the MPR for improving this situation; and
4. the possible influence of private animal production at this stage.

For two reasons the fourth point is of great interest:

1. Although considerable information is already available on the system of personal and subsidiary farming in the USSR and Eastern Europe, our knowledge about the situation and importance of this sector in the MPR is rather scanty.
2. Parallel to the 'normalization' of the political and economical relations between the MPR and China (PR of China) more information about the (positive) results of agricultural reforms in China will spread from the Chinese autonomous province of Inner Mongolia into the MPR. This might effect agricultural policy of the Mongolian Communist party in a way which makes a kind of 'de-collectivization' not unthinkable. All the more so, as Soviet media have begun commenting positively on the Chinese agricultural reforms.[1] This might enable the Mongolian leaders to embark on a more liberal agricultural policy.

General parameters of agricultural production

The territory of the MPR extends over 1.57 million square kilometres and thereby is roughly as large as the whole of continental Western Europe, excluding Scandinavia and Spain, and by one-third larger than neighbouring Inner Mongolia, which forms an Autonomous Region of China. Its location is somewhat more to the South than that of Europe (excluding the Mediterranean countries) and in North America comparable to the area from Minnesota to Montana. Yet with many high mountain ranges and roughly four-fifths of the country situated more than 1,000 metres above sea level under a distinctively continental climate, the natural endowment is unfavourable for arable agriculture and intensive livestock husbandry. Mongolian summers are short and hot, the winters dry and very cold. Average rainfall is 200–250 millimetres (80–90 inches), from 400 mm in the north to only 100 mm (40 inches) in the south. The vegetation types vary from alpine desert or mountain forest in the north over various types of steppe to desert in the south.

Less than one per cent of the territory is arable and permanent crop land (1.26 million hectares according to the CMEA statistics), of which between 0.5–0.8 million hectares are in permanent use and with a tiny irrigated share. Most of this is sown to grain, exclusively spring grains. More than 80 per cent are pasture and 10 per cent forests and woodland. Hectare yields are low and vary greatly between regions and over time.

Although the population has doubled since 1960, its density of 1.2 inhabitants per square kilometre is much lower than of Inner Mongolia and also lower than that of the adjacent Soviet areas of Siberia (excluding their subpolar and polar parts). In 1986, 52 per cent of Mongolia's population were urban, of whom almost a quarter were in the capital Ulan-Bator (Ulaanbaatar). Ethnically, 87 per cent of the total population are Mongols. The share of the economically active population is rather low (37 per cent in 1985), which is due in part to the large share of children and juveniles. About 43 per cent of the employed population work in agriculture and forestry, only 15 per cent in industry and manufacturing.

The territorial administrative organization is by 21 aimaks (provinces), of which 3 urban, and by somons (districts) as the basic unit.

Mongolia's political leaders consider their country to be 'in the gradual change towards an agrarian-industrial state', which in actual fact is tantamount to being predominantly agrarian. The official figure of a 17–18 per cent contribution on the 1981–5 average (22 per cent in 1986) of agriculture and forestry to the national income (material net product) seems rather an understatement, especially if measured in terms of value added.

Under the circumstances given by nature, more than 80 per cent of Mongolian agriculture's output derives from livestock farming, which in the main is all-year nomadic herding on natural pasture. Sheep predominate (58 per cent of all livestock numbers), then come goats, horned cattle, horses and camels.

The course of collectivization

In Mongolian interpretation of the country's current history, economic backwardness usually is referred to as 'the main obstacle to the transformation of agriculture'.[2] This may in fact have been the main reason, although others certainly also played a role, among them periodical instabilities in the domestic and foreign policy situation, resistance of the nomadic 'arat' – the Mongolian term for the individual herdsman[3] – population, lack of experience in managing a collectivized nomadic livestock economy, etc. At any rate, full collectivization took place a quarter of a century later than in the Soviet Union and at roughly the same time as in Eastern Europe.

In chronological order, Mongolian (and also Soviet) publications of economic history define three main development stages of the transformation of agriculture. From 1921 up to the mid-1950s, 1955/6–1959 and 1959 onwards. However, the first of these periods summarizingly glosses over the peripeties during almost half a century, which in official retrospect merely is considered a time in which the 'main task' consisted in convincing the Mongol nomads (arats) of the merits of collective animal husbandry. Therefore the collectivization process is subsequently depicted in somewhat greater detail.

On the 'eve of the revolution' (communist takeover and declaration of independence from China in 1921) there were 200,000 arat households in what at that time was called Outer Mongolia and on 24 November 1924 was proclaimed the Mongolian People's Republic. On the average, each of them had about forty animals, sheep and goats for the most part; more than nine out of ten inhabitants of the country subsisted on animal husbandry. Land was nationalized already in 1921, but in a country with almost no arable farming, the significance of such a step was different from, and less significant than, in countries of predominant arable agriculture.

By the end of the 1920s, the process of dispossessing the 'secular and clerical feudal lords' was completed. They had accounted for 8 per cent (mainly lamaist monks) of the population and had owned roughly half the total livestock inventories, often herded by dependent arats. These herds were distributed among the arats. As a consequence, not only the average number of animals per household, but also the number of arat households increased.

During 1929–32, the years of collectivization in the Soviet Union, farming co-operatives (collectives) and communes were established and herds collectivized in a coercive way. In reaction, the arats slaughtered 7 million of their animals, and total herd numbers declined by 32 per cent during 1931 and 1932,[4] farms were dissolved, because they did not prove viable under the given circumstances. The first

State farms, mainly arable farms, were established in 1935.

The 1930s and 1940s saw the establishment of collective (co-operative) farms of an 'initial form', in most of which only work was collective, whereas animals and implements remained in private ownership and were only temporarily used for the collective. Income was distributed according to work performed and also to provision of animals and implements for the collective. Ninety-one such co-operative associations with a total of 2,000 members are said to have existed in 1940.

In 1942, an 'Agricultural Model Statute' was decreed.[5] It provided for centralized collective (co-operative) farms, but was silent on the number of animals permitted for private ownership of members and also on the obligatory minimum of work to be performed for the collective. The period from the mid-1940s to the mid-1950s is depicted as one of strengthening the arat production associations of a 'half-socialized' form. For 1954, the share of arat households in various types of Agricultural Producer Associations (AA) is indicated at only 7 per cent and that of collectivized animals at 4.3 per cent.[6]

In 1954, the Twelfth Congress of the Mongolian People's Revolutionary Party decided on measures for implementing 'full collectivization'. A new Model Statute for Agricultural Associations was enacted in March, 1955.[7] The years up to 1959 represent the period of 'mass' collectivization.

By the end of 1959, 99.3 per cent of all arat households are included in Agricultural Associations and are called 'arat co-operators'.[8] At the December, 1959 plenary session of the Party Central Committee it was stated that the Mongolian agriculture had become socialist.

Soviet agriculture as a model

In past policy and developments in Mongolian agriculture, trends towards 'new developments' cannot be discerned. The Mongolian People's Revolutionary Party (MPRP) never denied Lenin's so-called Agricultural Co-operative Plan and the Soviet experience in collectivized agriculture as a model for Mongolia's ways of social reforms. It is useless to discuss whether there ever was a chance for the MPRP to go independent ways; too great has been the country's dependence on the USSR in politics and economics. Still, a certain difference between Mongolian and Russian agricultural developments consists in the longer time-span it took the Mongolian communists from their assuming political power in the early 1920s to the point of their starting agricultural collectivization in the late 1950s. Even if abstracting from the Soviet Marxist interpretation of history, according to which Mongolia 'on its way from feudalism to socialism skipped over the development of capitalism' one finds no fundamental differences between the socialized agriculture of the MPR

71

and the Russian model, neither in content nor in form or in the social-economical issues of agricultural policy, except its adaptation to livestock husbandry on vast pasture lands.

The Marxism-based presentation of modern Mongolia's history gives 1959 as the year of the 'victory of socialism in the countryside', when, according to the official version, about 360,000 private small herdsmen with their family members 'voluntarily' associated in collectives or Agricultural Associations (AA).[9] The term voluntary, which is used by official communist institutions, cannot be taken at face value. It is disproved, among other things, by the outcome of earlier attempts of the Communist Party at establishing so-called lower forms of agricultural collectives, the production associations, which upto the mid-1950s all ended in economic failure. Thus, the mass slaughter of animals in 1931–2 (see above) happened when in 1930 'leftists' of the Communist Party spread the slogan 'Mongolia is now ready for the collectivization of agriculture'. The number of co-operative arat households remained small up to the mid-1950s.

Today, after almost thirty years of existence, socialized agriculture in Mongolia seems to have stabilized in its institutional, ideological and organizational aspects. To a foreign observer the similarities between the Soviet and Mongolian agricultural systems are obvious. They exist in the following fields:

1. typical organizational forms like State farms, collective farms, inter-collective farms and private subsidiary farms;
2. labour organization as well as labour policy;
3. social security system and income-policy;
4. procurement system for agricultural produce and price policy; and
5. centralized planning and administration of agriculture.

For a short period even so-called machine-animal-husbandry-stations existed, with tasks assigned similar to those performed in the USSR by the machine-tractor-stations up to 1958/9. Finally, there was the parallel of a period during which economically weak AAs were annexed to State farms or had to amalgamate, with the result that the number of collective farms dropped from the original 354 (1960) to 255 (up to 1986).

As a counterpart, the number of State farms (twenty-five in 1960) had increased to fifty-two by 1985 as a consequence of new ones being established. It is important, however, that Mongolia's collective farm sector still accounts for 70 to 75 per cent of the total agricultural output and for more than two-thirds (68 per cent) of all agricultural workers. Thus, in contrast to the USSR and Cuba, but similar to the other countries with socialized agriculture, it plays a dominant role. This seems to be mainly a result of the geographically conditioned orientation on animal production.

Natural endowment and climate acted towards immense sizes of enterprises as far as land area and livestock numbers are concerned, which is unique among CMEA countries. In most cases the territory of one AA coincides with that of one somon (district). Its agriculturally used area covers 450,000 hectares on average and basically consists of pasture used with low intensity. Still, with an average of about 61,500 animal units per AA, the herds are no larger than they were in the early 1960s, and this in spite of the number of AAs having dropped since then. This fact reveals difficulties in animal production, which will be dealt with below.

Somehow it is typical for the structure of production in Mongolia's agriculture that one finds a kind of division of labour in the major fields of production between state farms and AAs, where the State farms mostly deal with growing crops, including feed in specialized State enterprises, and raising breeding stocks whereas the AAs concentrate on animal production and do very little crop production.

The agricultural population

As in the Soviet Union and the other socialist states, people employed in state farms and feed producing enterprises and, as long as they existed, in machine-animal-husbandry-stations, are considered workers or employees of the State. Like those in urban places they are paid tariff wages and premiums and receive social transfer incomes. The remuneration of arats for collective works is largely dependent on the economic results of their AA in a given year.

The arats consist of the formerly private livestock breeders (herdsmen) who formed Agricultural Associations in 1959. By now, the generation of their descendants is taking their place, who know about the former agrarian conditions only by hearsay and are ideologically influenced by the way the party pictures that earlier life. Improved earning and working possibilities in industry and better urban living conditions seem to be major reasons for this development, their occupational and emotional ties with agriculture and rural life seem to vanish more and more. The result is a shortage of agricultural workers, which the Communist Youth Association of Mongolia tries to counter by imposing the obligation of agricultural work every year on thousands of young people.

The total number of member households of the Agricultural Associations – in most cases both spouses are members if a married couple is concerned – is estimated to exceed 200,000. They represent about 80 per cent of the people in agricultural occupations, and one third of total employment in the Mongolian economy at large. Together with their family members (children under 16 years of age) and retired old people they represent the largest group among the rural population (approximately 720,000 out of a total of 900,000 in 1985).

Thus, the arats determine the characteristical 'profile' of Agricultural Associations and rural communities from the social, economical and intellectual point of view. For most of them life is that of traditional nomadism. As it is said in an arat report: 'On the search for the best pasture grounds the herdsmen change the yurt camps sixteen to seventeen times a year, moving distances of 600 to 700 kilometres.[10]

As to ownership of herds, the situation of the arat in pre-revolutionary times was not wholly different from that prevailing today. Although the available data are not fully compatible, they do indicate that roughly half of the total livestock numbers belonged to the nobility and the religious institutions, similar to the share of AAs of today and was tended by the arats, while the rest was owned by the arats themselves.

Disproportions between food production and population growth

According to official Mongolian announcements, published in such sources as 'Novosti Mongolii', Mongolia's agriculture of today is a prosperous branch of the national economy, with great importance for the society as a whole, although the main expansion occurred in branches like raw material production, industry and services. According to statements of party leaders, Mongolia is now able to cover its agricultural requirements in all important raw materials – including grain – by own resources and even to export growing quantities of animal products. According to the party, the standard of living of the arats and the workers in the countryside has also improved, and good results have been achieved in extending educational and health services to the central settlements of the arats.

It is true that during the last three decades the social situation of the nearly one million rural inhabitants (in 1986 accounting for 48 per cent of the total population) has somewhat improved if compared to the first half of the century as far as standard of living and daily work-life are concerned. This emerges also from the fact that the average life expectancy of Mongolian people is sixty-six years, as compared to only about thirty 'before the Revolution'.[11] Measured against the official party targets, however, these achievements remain far below the promises. Mongolia remains one of the poorest and underdeveloped countries in the CMEA.

The lagging of the growth of agricultural production behind the population growth is one of the main reasons of this state of affairs. In particular, animal production is regularly missing the planned targets. If it were not for the better development of crop production with its high growth rates, the general situation of Mongolian agriculture would be much worse. By the mid-1980s, the strained situation in the supply of food in Mongolia has entered a critical phase, as can be demonstrated by some global figures.

With an annual average growth of 3 per cent (1960–80) and 2.6 per cent more recently (1981–5), Mongolia's population more than doubled during the last three decades (the figure was expected to reach 2 million in the autumn of 1987, compared with 952,000 in 1960), whereas agricultural production grew by only about half, the livestock production alone even less, by roughly 40 per cent.[12] The population growth in Mongolia is going to continue, and Mongolian demographers estimate that by the end of our century the number may reach the 3 million mark.[13]

The lag between agricultural production and population development led to declining consumption per head in meat and milk. Both foods have traditionally been, and still are, essential elements of nutrition in Mongolia in general and for the rural consumers in particular, although the structure of their nutrition is changing to greater consumption of grain products, potatoes, sugar and vegetables. The following figures give an impression of the decline. In the early 1960s the consumption of meat per head was 125 kg, one of the highest in the world. Now it has fallen to 91 kg (average for 1981–4) – that is, by 27 per cent – and will at best keep this level in the next few years. At the same time, milk consumption per head also dropped by about one-fifth between 1970 (185 kg; milk and milk products including butter in terms of fresh milk) and the mid-1980s (149 kg on average in 1981–4).[14]

Tentatively estimated other consumption figures, although apparently below those of Eastern Europe and Cuba, do not compare badly with those of Vietnam and China, so that the overall calories and protein intake may seem physiologically more or less adequate. Yet the important point is that they have been markedly declining during the past decade, while incomes rose, so that demand is less and less being met and popular dissatisfaction is likely to mount.

Regardless of the decline in domestic food supplies, Mongolia depends on the export of considerable quantities of agricultural products, especially slaughter animals, meat and other animal products, in order to pay its imports of investment goods as well as of certain processed foods (e.g. sugar, vegetable oil, vegetables, fruit, fish and tea). One may guess that, in addition, Mongolia has to feed the estimated 70,000 Soviet soldiers stationed in the country. (They may be being withdrawn recently.)

The main causes for the situation as outlined are the stagnation in herd numbers and the disappointing development of animal productivity. For example, the number of livestock in the socialist sector of agriculture went down by 13 per cent[15] between 1981 and 1985. Neglecting the herd structure by kinds of animals, as the Mongolian statistics do in global statements,[16] the total figure in 1985 (21.98 million) was about 0.7 per cent smaller than it had been when the collectivization of agriculture started in 1959. Remarkably, in spite of the expansion of the veterinary system, of the construction of winter stables, of artificial water supply and an improved fodder production, the losses of animals are still high.

One of the reasons are the extremely cold, often very snowy winters in combination with a shortage of fodder and the lack of stables for the animals. For instance, in the winter of 1986–7, because of unfavourable climatic conditions, more than 6 million – about 30 per cent of the total herds – had to be moved from their pasture areas to other parts of the country, which is bound to have caused losses.[17] Even in 1985, which was supposed to be a normal year, the agricultural co-operatives lost 830,000 young and 920,000 adult animals, equal to the total livestock numbers of 27 AAs, according to a Mongolian source.[18]

Obviously, it is not only the unfavourable climatic conditions combined with the economic underdevelopment which make protection against a harsh nature so difficult and have prevented significant progress until now. It is also the socio-economic and political system which sometimes reinforces these difficulties.

During the Sixth National Congress of the AA in October 1986 some of the systematic shortcomings were named, such as:

1. permanent monitoring of farms and agricultural enterprises by the Party and the administration;
2. outmoded planning methods;
3. low incentives for the farms and enterprises and also for their workers;
4. inefficient labour organization and low labour morale; and
5. underestimation of social components of policy, in other words, of the 'human factor'.

In addition to this, official labour policy worked counter-productively because it was for too long orientated mainly towards the requirements of industry and not those of agriculture. It formed an additional impulse for rural–urban migration as a consequence of bad living and working conditions in the countryside. Governmental actions to supply agriculture with the needed number of skilled workers have proven ineffective.

Reforms the Soviet way

The shortcomings outlined above and some more of today are held responsible by the party for the 'negative developments' in agriculture during recent years.

Referring to the developments in the Soviet Union – with a time lag of about two or three years – reforms for Mongolian agricultural policy have also been discussed in Ulan Bator since 1986. The issues are intensification of agricultural production by specialization and concentration. They are tied in with quantitative and qualitative aspects supposed to reduce the very unfavourable dependency on climatic factors. The discussions and proceedings of reform were mirrored in the 'Programme of the Development of Agriculture and Improved Food Supply of the Population' (Food Programme; 1985) for the period from 1986 up to the year 2000. The programme has been developed with the strong support of Russian advisors and is very similar to the Soviet 'Food Programme' of 1982 as far as issues and methods are concerned.

The reform issues in Mongolian agriculture that were mainly discussed can be summarized like this: reduction of centralized economy; more autonomy for local administration and farm management; better material incentives for the arats; and improved social services of the State in agriculture.

As in Moscow, where various agricultural ministries and top agencies were combined into the 'State Committee for the Agro-industrial Complex/Gosagroprom', the ministries for agriculture and for agricultural water supply in Ulan Bator were merged and a certain amount of employees dismissed. Economic indicators shall now play the most important role in farm management, for instance through the introduction of cost accounting. A reform of the agricultural labour organization and a new system making wages dependent of productive performance is also in preparation. The reforms do not really differ very much from those in the USSR, except that they are modified for Mongolian requirements. As the Russian reform discussions are widely known, their Mongolian counterparts need not be discussed in detail. The implementation of the reforms in Mongolia will depend indirectly on the results of those in the Soviet Union. Without doubt, putting them into practice will be harder and will need more time in Mongolia because the requirements for a quantitatively and qualitatively market-orientated agricultural production are very much conditioned upon infrastructure and cadres; and the shortcomings in these fields are more grave than in the Soviet Union.

A positive influence on this development might be exerted by the 'Inter Co-operative Associations', which have been established since the beginning of the current decade and numbered thirty-six by 1986. These associations are a kind of service enterprises for the AA, they produce feed, provide transport and are engaged in the construction of houses and farm buildings. One of their expected advantages is a more efficient handling of investments as well as a greater machinery and labour capacity.

Support and tolerance for the private ('personal') subsidiary farming of the population and labour organization by 'family links' are other traits reminding of the Soviet reforms, to be dealt with below.

Private plots – the Mongolian way

An obviously more benevolent official attitude towards the private subsidiary plot and animal production represents a new accentuation in Mongolian agrarian policy. However, it is not a specifically Mongolian 'new way' in the meaning of the word, as its development is closely related to the overall political situation of today and is part of a trend, which can be observed in all CMEA countries in their dealing with private economic activities.

This new accentuation is valid for Mongolia, too, and finds its expression in a changed approach to private agricultural production. Until the late 1970s, such production was looked upon as merely a subsistence sector for the arats. Since the Agricultural Associations are economically unable to provide the arats with a sufficient subsistence from their work in the collective economy – a problem still existing – provision of food and additional income is now expected to result from subsidiary plot and animal farming. For example, the setting of lower maximum limits for private animal husbandry as desired by parts of the party in 1967, when the new Model Charter was being discussed, was rejected by the former head of the party, Y. Tsedenbal, on the grounds that the collective economy of the AA is not yet able to secure a sufficient subsistence for its members.[19]

This argument still serves as an ideological justification of private production in agriculture, but its main significance is viewed under the potential contribution the sector can make to improving the overall supply of food. The further development of private subsidiary farming as desired by the party obviously exceeds the present possibilities as well as the willingness of the arats. This is made obvious by the party's criticism that private livestock holdings per family usually are well below the upper level approved in the Model Charter. A major exhibition in the capital city of Ulan Bator in the autumn of 1986 was meant to promote private subsidiary farming by a presentation of its achievements. It probably was the first exhibition of this kind in a CMEA country. The very same purpose is aimed at by the efforts of the party and government to improve the selling possibilities for private producers, for instance by organizing and improving local markets and by raising the State procurement prices for such products. In the Mongolian 'Food Programme' it is mentioned that the private subsidiary farms should produce in the near future up to 35 to 40 per cent of the total production of meat and dairy products.[20]

The Constitution and the Model Charter (1967) entitles the members of

AAs to private agricultural production, in this case to the ownership of livestock. The Model Charter, deals with the rules for pasturing in the sense that the arats get a share of the pasture land, the location of which is changing and marked off from public pasture, without commenting on its size. More recent rules, however, for the use of land for private crop production are contained in the 'Law concerning usage of land' (1971). They will not be discussed any further here. This 'land law' (Article 18) states, that the arats are not assigned permanent pasture areas on an individual basis, but are entitled to graze their animals on the pasture grounds of the AA. Because of the fact that the work required for grazing the private together with the overall livestock herds cannot amount to much, the 'operating costs' for private animal production are all in all low. It seems that the arats do not have to pay taxes on their private livestock, but since the end of the 1970s are under an obligation to sell certain numbers of animal products to the government.[21]

The permitted numbers of animal holdings in private ownership depend on the quality of the given pasture land and prevailing other conditions. In Northern Mongolia with its steppe pasture and a relatively good vegetation, called 'Khangai zone' after the nearby mountain range, the upper limit is fifty animals per family household, whereas it is seventy-five animals in the 'Gobi zone'. Usually the actual limits applied are per member of a given arat family, with up to ten animals in the northern, and fifteen in the southern part of the country for each person. Since families not rarely comprise ten or more children, the latter rules may lead to actual animal numbers per family, which are undesirably large in the eyes of the political regime. This is why the mentioned upper limits exist. The Model Charter states that illegally kept animals are to be sold to either Agricultural Associations or the State. As a rule, however, the actual numbers remain below those limits.

In contrast to regulations in other CMEA countries, there are no special instructions in Mongolia as to the kinds of animals permitted within the numerical limits. The Model Charter only states that cattle, horses and camels must not make up more than one-third of the total private holding in terms of all kinds of animals owned per family. Since the production of pigs and poultry is to be enlarged for reasons of food policy, no upper limit exists for these animals. Every arat family presently owns 32.4 animals on average; a little more than 20 of them (63 per cent) are sheep (14 head) and goats (6.6 head). Along with sheep and goats, every household owns about five horses, which are mainly used for riding and working (for instance to transport the one or two yurts that are owned by every family and to produce milk of the mares), as well as six head of cattle.

It is hard to tell why the arats privately keep animal numbers well below the upper limits set in the Model Charter. Declining interest in private animal production, for whatever reason, is definitely not the

Table 3.1 Livestock numbers by farm categories (thousands at end of year)

	1950	1960	1970	1980	1983	1984	1985	1986	1981–85 average: 1960 (per cent)
I. Total numbers (all farm categories)									
Cattle[a]	1 988	1 906	2 108	2 397	2 374	2 374	2 408	2 480	+ 25.1
of which cows[b]	776	795	871	1 010	1 006	984	1 007	1 019	+ 25.8
Sheep	12 575	12 102	13 312	14 231	14 110	13 391	13 249	13 194	+ 16.4
Goats	4 979	5 631	4 204	4 567	5 548	4 298	4 299	4 401	− 20.0
Horses	2 317	2 503	2 318	1 985	1 960	1 961	1 971	2 018	− 20.8
II. Socialist sector[c]									
Cattle[a]	37	1 115	1 040	1 444	1 393	1 368	1 359	1 380	+ 25.0
of which cows[b]	19[d]	466	451	650	644	625	631	642	+ 36.9
Sheep	178	9 558	11 319	12 556	12 182	11 392	11 179	11 042	+ 27.2
Goats	16	4 769	3 232	3819	3 641	3 339	3 246	3 281	− 24.7
Horses	124	1 614	1 422	293	1 232	1 216	1 207	1 209	− 22.7
III. Private ('personal') farms of the population									
Cattle[a]	1 971	790	1 068	953	981	1 006	1 049	1 008	+ 25.3
of which cows[b]	685[d]	330	420	359	363	359	376	396	+ 9.9
Sheep	12 395	2 544	1 993	1 675	1 928	1 999	2 070	2 154	− 24.3
Goats	4 963	862	862	747	907	960	1 034	1 120	+ 5.6
Horses	2 193	888	896	693	728	745	764	809	− 17.5

Sources: Statistical Yearbooks of the Council for Mutual Economic Assistance (CMEA), Moscow.
a Including buffalos and yaks. b Including buffalo cows and yak cows. c State farms and Agricultural Co-operatives. d 1952.

Table 3.2 Meat production and percentage of private ('personal') meat production (1000 t and per cent)

	1960	1970	1975	1980	1983	1984	1985	1986	1983–86 average: 1960 (per cent)
I. Meat production,[a] total	185	180	235	227	230	233	226	240	+25.5
of which: beef	62.3	51.7	60.6	70.6	68.1	68.2	68.1	75.3	+12.2
mutton and goat's meat	96.2	95.9	132	116	124	126	116	123	+27.1
II. Meat production[a] of the socialist sector	110	124	171	167	172	177	164	177	+56.8
of which: beef	28.7	23.7	30.8	36.2	37.2	38.1	36.2	41.1	+32.9
mutton and goat's meat	62.6	77.9	115	102	108.8	111.6	99.9	106.2	+70.3
III. Meat production[b] of private producers	75	56	64	60	58	56	62	63	−20.4
in per cent of total	40.5	31.1	27.2	26.6	25.2	24	27.4	26.2	—
of which: beef	33.6	28	29.8	34.4	30.9	30.1	31.9	34.2	− 5.5
mutton and goat's meat	33.6	18.0	17.0	14.0	15.2	14.4	16.1	16.8	−53.5

Source: Statistical Yearbooks of the Council for Mutual Economic Assistance (CMEA), Moscow.
a Meat and fat in slaughter weight. b Derived as residuals.

motive, because in earlier years the private livestocks also were well below (thirty-three in the early 1960s compared to thirty-one animals in the early 1970s). The main reason might be the general shortage of feed as well as the high losses of animals, that prevent the numbers to exceed a certain limit.

Allegedly there are also arats, who increase their total private livestock far beyond the legal limits.[22]

About one-fifth (21 per cent) of the total livestock numbers in Mongolia are privately owned, as opposed to approximately 30 per cent in the early 1960s, soon after collectivization. In 1986 the arats owned a high share of horses (40 per cent of the total) and of cattle (44 per cent) whereas the percentages for sheep (16 per cent) and goats (25 per cent) are much smaller (Table 3.1). The private producers generate more than a quarter of the total meat production (see Table 3.2) and up to 40 per cent of milk and butter produced in Mongolia, of which significant quantities are consumed by the arat families themselves. Including other products, such as wool and hides, the private contribution to total animal production in Mongolia makes up one third or more.[23]

These figures demonstrate the existential importance the contribution of the subsidiary farming of the arats has for the supply of the people and the industry with animal products. It also explains the particular interest of the party in the further development of private animal production.

'Family links' as the basis of animal production

'Family links' as they are lately being discussed and introduced in the USSR, have been existing in Mongolia since the earliest days of socialized agriculture. They are a result of the specific Mongolian conditions in animal production of the Agricultural Associations and within these represent the basic element of labour organization. Such links consist of workgroups of one to two, more often two to three arat families, which range through the pasture lands with the grazing animals they are responsible for. These workgroups are called 'Suur' in Mongolian, which can be translated 'base'. Usually the families, that make up a 'Suur' are akin to each other (for instance several generations of one family), so that it is legitimate also to define them as 'family-business' under the aspect of group relations and self-reliant work.

The economic function of the much bigger production brigades, of which there are two or three within one AA, as well as of the 'sections' mentioned sometimes, are not to be discussed at this point. Among their functions is the role of representing outposts of the central administration of the Agricultural Associations and fulfilling supply functions for the more than 30,000 herding camps.[24] Most important perhaps is their role in co-ordination and planning and maybe also controlling.

Typical for the work of a co-operative arat is his combining the collective with the private work of a herdsman. The statutory grazing of privately owned animals on pasture marked off from that of the collective seems to be more symbolic than real. Who of the far distant central farm management office will ever check whether privately owned sheep and cattle are in fact kept on separate pasture grounds? Such control is also rendered near to impossible by the frequent change of pasture grounds over hundreds of kilometres.

The animals of arats and of the Agricultural Associations are marked by ear marks and brands, but the Mongolian media often mention that arats sometimes exchange their own sick animals for healthy ones of the AA. The use of pasture areas and the supply of water to the privately-owned animals are free of charge for the arats. To what extent the arats can use the collective winter stables and veterinarian services and what they are charged for this is unknown to the author.

The free use of pastures and watering points in essence is a payment in kind by the AA, which has to be taken into account, when the relatively low wages of the arats or else the contribution of private husbandry to overall livestock production are considered.

Thus, concerning the daily work of an arat, the technique of pasture changing, of fodder and water supply and generally of the responsibility for the herd, there are no big differences between the time before the collectivization and after.

At present, the herds are bigger and specialized into species and by age, as distinct from earlier times, when the so-called private arats strove – among other things out of reasons of risk-balancing – to keep the five main species in their herds. The grazing of today, it is true, is based on a better infrastructure (e.g., veterinarian services, greater numbers of artesian wells, planned feed provision for the winter and arrangements for winter stables, improved communications and a weather forecast system) compared with earlier times. On the other hand, Mongolian statements claiming that mechanization has entered pasture management still remains propaganda.

For the central authorities in the AA one as yet unsolved problem of the 'family-business' in the Suur camps is the limited possibility of control. The work of an arat, compared with that of the Soviet kolkhoznik, is characterized much more by independence and self-reliance. But it may seem that a decline of discipline has spread among the arats. Just recently the Mongolian party leader Jambyn Batmunkh assumed the high losses of animals to be caused by the fact that 'in numerous areas the grazing-rules are infringed upon by leaving the herds without almost any care'.[25] In reaction to this phenomenon the party shows a tendency to fusion more Suur ('family-business') and make them more dependent on brigades and AA-authorities in organizational matters. The official reason given is the aim to improve efficiency as well as working and living conditions of the arat families, but more effective control over private animal production may also be a motive.

It is questionable, however, whether the reorganization of the traditional labour units by forming larger working groups is the best way to elicit more responsibility and discipline. Both seem well-developed as far as the animals owned privately by the arats are concerned. There are signs that losses are lower and animal productivity is higher in private than in collective herds. As a consequence, the party will have to look for ways to increase the 'material incentives' of the arats for collective work. Faster and more successful could be the road already taken of improving the conditions for private animal production.

Income and expenditure of arats

Income

I could not get representative statistics about level, structure and development of arat incomes for their 250 obligatory work-days in the AA a year. Some single items, however, range from 3,000 tughrigs a year[26] to 10,000–12,000, including often a certain amount of bonus payments. The earnings of a shepherd in Western Mongolia (Choibalsan Agricultural Association, Bulgan District), who makes over 16,000 tughrigs annually, including wages and a bonus for additional fattening of animals and for overfulfilling the plan targets is without doubt an exceptional case, but it indicates that income disparities within the arat group are considerable.[27] An annual per worker income of 10,000 tughrigs (about 3,000 US dollars at the official exchange rate in 1986) has to be regarded a top income, as the average earning was only 3,200 tughrigs (960 US dollars) by about 1985.[28] Even the latter figure is ten times higher than in 1959 (312 tughrigs) and went through 2,400 tughrigs at the end of the 1970s. Due to a Russian source of 1982,[29] private animal production contributed 20 per cent to the annual money income of the arats. Related to the figure mentioned above for 1979 this is about 500 tughrigs a year. The relatively small amount confirms the implicit assumption, that the main part of private animal production is consumed by the arats themselves, and only a small part is marketed.

Depending on the value at which the family requirements covered by animal products are rated, the total annual income of an arat corresponds – or at least will be close – to the State guaranteed minimum wage of 6,000 tughrigs a year set for workers and employees in other branches of the economy. It has to be added, however, that the personal income of an arat from animal products at least in part results from additional work put in by members of his family, so that by working hours it still would be far below that of other segments of the working population. We have no precise informations about the income relationship between arats and state-farm workers. According to Mongolian sources, the money income of the arats stays far behind that of the farm workers. As in the Soviet Union, efforts are made also to approximate the income of arats to the farm workers' level and in the long-term to lift the rural incomes generally to the level of urban and industrial workers.

According to Mongolian media reports about the living standard of the arats, private animal production supplies arat families with nearly all necessities of nutrition and enables them to spend most of their income for purchased non-food products. If such reports are correct, private production would indeed be indispensable for the arat population, that is, for more than one-third of the nation.

Especially with the younger arats of the emerging new generation, the question of material and immaterial benefits of private animal production in a socialized economy gain in importance. The main private sector products are meat, fats, milk, wool, hides and sheepskins. How many of them are consumed within the arat families and which part goes into local markets or is sold to State trade organizations is not exactly known. But in view of the usually big size of arat families and the low animal productivity, the share of products being sold should be small. In addition, the development of local food markets has just started and already is impeded by the weak transportation and trade infrastructure.

As mentioned above, people's diet in present-day Mongolia is supplemented by more food of vegetable origin than in former times. Nevertheless, meat and milk products remain the most substantial element of nutrition, especially for the arats. Their average consumption is far above the country's average – due to the existence of private animal production. The urgency to supply the arat families with those substantial foods requires carrying on with private animal production.

Applying expense structure patterns of comparable CMEA countries to the share of spending for food in Mongolia, these have to be assessed at least at one-third if not two-fifths or more of the total expenses of a rural resident. If most of this is derived from private animal production, its contribution to the total income of an arat (cash and foods, recalculated in money) is very sizeable, indeed. Such an assessment corresponds with a recent Mongolian information, which says that the share of income from work in the AA is 65 per cent of the total annual income of an arat.[30] Accordingly, private livestock holdings and other kinds of agricultural and non-agricultural productions and activities (and probably also monetary social transfers) roughly contribute the remaining 35 per cent to the income (after about 50 per cent in 1972).

Household expenditures

Due to the targets of the 'Food Programme', incomes according to work performance in the AA shall rise about 50 to 60 per cent until the end of the century. This brings up the question of the purchasing power of the arat's income, that is, the development of their living standard.

Statistical data about retail prices (level, price-relations, development) are not available. On the basis of actual Mongolian media reports, it may be assumed that the incomes of arats – like those of collective farm members in the Soviet Union – exceed the availability of those consumer goods which they would like to buy with a view to quantity as well as to quality. The reasons for this are both:

1. the general shortage of consumer durables; and
2. the worse supply with goods to the countryside in comparison to the 'urban' and industrial zones.

The supply of services also is far below potential demand. Party leaders several times criticized the shortage of consumer goods, and of means for private production of the arats in particular, that is, building materials and farm equipment. Their supply does not seem to have improved. A strong demand exists among the village people for motorbicycles, radios, TV sets, sewing machines and modern yurts. Mongolian specification of goods demanded by the arats, but not available in the needed quantity and quality, lists the following items: Tent canvas, felt and other articles for the construction of yurts, petrol tanks, cream separators, riding-horse saddles, and warm boots.

The deficient supply of goods to arats' demand may well be one of the main reasons for their low labour motivation and also be responsible for the fact that the arats do no expand their private livestock number up to the permitted upper limits. If they did, the income derived from selling produce exceeding their own consumption would not sizeably contribute to improving their living standard because of the mentioned shortage of consumer goods. Still other Mongolian media announcements imply a certain rising of prosperity of the rural population. Thus, it has been said that between the mid-1970s and the early 1980s almost half of the arat families (40 per cent) bought modern yurts, and that there is a general tendency to have two yurts in a family.[31] At the beginning of the 1980s about half of Mongolia's inhabitants lived in yurts, which still are preferred also by part of the urban population. The price of a yurt seems to be of the order of 3,500 tughrigs,[32] which is roughly the annual average income of an arat.

Outlook

In a speech of summer, 1987, to representatives of the Mongolian People's Revolution Party, Shambyn Batmunkh, the party leader, announced that market-economy mechanisms after the model of the Soviet Union will be introduced. According to the Beijing news agency Xinhua,[33] he made an appeal to learn from the Soviet economic reform. In the future the enterprises should plan their production in own responsibility and act with a view to profitability.

The targets of the 'Food Programme' are nearly to double agricultural production (plus 80 per cent) and to raise meat production by about 30 per cent until the end of the century. The party leaders know that these goals cannot be reached with the outmoded methods of planning and administration. That is why Mongolia, in following the Soviet example, started reforms in agriculture. Granting more autonomy for farm management is meant to increase productivity and the economic results of the AAs.

At this stage, it is not possible to make statements or prognoses about the further development and results of the reforms. At any rate, a stronger reliance on the individual interest is discernible, be it through 'family links' or through tolerance towards private ('personal') animal husbandry.

The deficiencies of food supply in Mongolia forced the party to change its policy with regard to the private subsidary sector. The private producers are not only tolerated, but in various ways even get assistance and material support in order to help them to contribute a greater share to the nation's agricultural output. Due to the strong population growth in coming years and to the low efficiency of socialized agriculture, which can be expected to continue for some time to come, there will be good prospects for the future production development of the private agricultural sector. Whether the planned reform measures will motivate the arats to enlarge the private livestock inventories beyond the present level, will mainly depend on the level of the prices of agricultural products on the one hand and on the supply of the arats with consumer goods on the other.

It may be assumed that the reforms in Chinese agriculture will effect the further agrarian policy of Mongolia. Yet, the time and the intensity of these effects seem difficult to estimate.

Notes and References

For valuable comments, suggestions and indications of additional sources I want to thank Mr. Alan Sanders, Reading, England.

A note on sources: The present paper is based mainly on information published since the mid-1970s as contained in the Russian-language newspaper *Novosti Mongolii* (for source references abbreviated NM), issued by the Mongolian agency MONTSAME at Ulan Bator (Ulaanbatar), and on

the English-language periodical *Mongolia*, which also appears at Ulan
Bator. In addition, the rich inventories of Soviet publications on Mongolia,
which are available at the Zentrum fuer Kontinentale Agrar- und
Wirtschaftsforschung of the Justus Liebig University at Giessen (Federal
Republic of Germany), were used. Other source material was found in
German – Federal Republic as well as GDR – monographs on Mongolia,
most of them of an earlier time, and in relevant articles and reports in
German newspapers and periodicals and also in English-language
information papers.

1. In an interview with *Frankfurter Allgemeine Zeitung*, 11 July 1987, the
   director of the Institute for the Economy of the Socialist World System
   in Moscow, O.T. Bogomolov, described the agrarian policy of
   Hungary and the People's Republic of China as 'exemplary' for the
   Soviet Union.
2. For example by Zhadambaa S, Sharaval'di Sh., (1966)
   Sel'skokhoziaistvennye kooperativy Mongol'skoi Narodnoi Respubliki,
   Ulaan-Baatar: 18. – The subsequent periodization and its facts are
   taken from this Mongolian source published in Russian, English and
   Mongolian and also from the following Russian monographs:

   Akademiia Nauk SSSR/Institut Narodov Azii (ed.) (1969) *Ocherki
   ekonomiki Mongol'skoi Narodnoi Respubliki*, Moscow: 3–76.
   Bavrin E.P. (1984) *Mongol'skaia Narodnaia Republika*, Moscow:
   12–34
   Pisarev V.I. (1968) *Sel'skoe khoziaistvo Mongol'skoi Narodnoi
   Respubliki*, Moscow: 19–47.
   Ulimzhiev D.B. *Sotsialisticheskoe pereustrojstvo sel'skogo khoziastva v
   MNR*, Ulan Ude: 22–196.

3. In Mongolia, agricultural workers often are collectively called arats. In
   the present paper the name 'arat' refers to herdsmen only.
4. Akademiia Nauk SSR (ed.) (1954) *Istoriia Mongol'skoi Narodnoi
   Respubliki*, Moscow: 287.
5. Akademiia Nauk SSSR/Institut Narodov Azii (ed.) (1969): 22, 23.
6. Akademiia Nauk SSSR/Institut Narodov Azii (ed.) (1969): 23.
7. Pisarev (1968): 37 (see note 2).
8. Akademiia Nauk SSSR/Institut Narodov Azii (ed.) (1969): 24.
9. *Narodnoe khoziaistvo MNR za 40 let*, Ulan Bator 1961: 47, 89:
   'Number of members of the Agricultural Associations in 1959
   (September 1) 360,100'. See Akademiia Nauk SSSR/Institut Narodov
   Azii (1969): 24.
10. Report of an arat living in the province Ubsa-Nur in North-west
    Mongolia, near the border to the Russian Altai-region.
11. *Novosti Mongolii*, 11, August 1987.
12. 'Mongolian Agriculture Today and Tomorrow', *Mongolia*, Ulan Bator,
    1/1987: 10
13. *Novosti Mongolii*, 2 September 1986.

14. *National Economy MPR 1973*, Ulan Bator: 65 and *Narodnoe khoziaistvo MNR 1984*, Ulan Bator, 1985: p. 26.
15. *Novosti Mongolii*, 31 October 1986.
16. Mongolian livestock statistics in their data, overall as well as regional ones and those for individual farms, generally do not make a distinction by kinds of animals. There is, however, a Mongolian recalculated livestock unit, called the 'bodo' where one head of cattle or a horse is taken at unity, one camel at 1.5 bodos, and seven sheep or else ten goats are equivalent to one bodo unit.
17. *Novosti Mongolii*, 20 March 1987.
18. *Novosti Mongolii*, 31 October 1986.
19. Quoted from Graivoronskii V.V. (1982) *Kooperirovannoe aratstvo MNR: Izmeneniia v urovne zhizni 1960–1980*, Moscow: 62.
20. *Novosti Mongolii*, 29 October 1985.
21. Sanders A. (1978) 'Mongolia lays down the law', *Far Eastern Economic Review'*, 26 May: 87.
22. Graivoronskii (1982): 63.
23. Author's estimate, based on the information of *Novosti Mongolii*, (26 March 1985) that Agricultural Associations account for about 60 per cent of the total animal production of Mongolia.
24. *Novosti Mongolii*, 23 June 1987.
25. *Novosti Mongolii*, 6 December 1986.
26. *Novosti Mongolii*, 25 October 1986. Tughrig is the Mongolian monetary unit – 1 tughrig = 0.30 US dollar at the official exchange rate of the State Bank in Ulan Bator (*Novosti Mongolii*, 19 September 1986).
27. Dulam L, (1987) 'Mongolian Villagers', *Mongolia*, p. 8. In the article the 'over 16,000 tughrigs' are valued at 'about 6,000 US dollars'.
28. *Novosti Mongolii*, 9 December 1986.
29. Quoted from Graivoronskii (1982): 100.
30. *Novosti Mongolii*, 5 February 1985.
31. *Bauern-Echo*, Berlin (East), 19 November 1980.
32. In a report on an Agricultural Association it is said that 'young men get 3,500 tughrigs to buy a new yurt after finishing military service', see: *Bauern-Echo*, 19 November 1980.
33. Chinese News Agency *Xinhua*, quoted by *Associated Press*, 2 July 1987.

Chapter four

Cuba: a unique variant of Soviet-type agriculture

Peter Gey

Introduction
Agrarian reform laws and integration plans
The brigade system on state farms
Collectivization of small land owners
Individual and collective plots
State and non-state agricultural commercialization
Between 'revolutionary offensive' and Soviet-orientated pragmatism

Introduction

Cuban agriculture in the period prior to the revolution was essentially characterized by sugar plantations (*latifundios*) and large cattle farms on the one hand, and small farms (*minifundios*) on the other. 9.4 per cent of the owners controlled 73.3 per cent of the land, while 66.1 per cent of the farm units held only 7.4 per cent of the land. (Chonchol, 1963: 72–3). After 1959, structural transformations were undertaken in order to redistribute land ownership and to integrate agricultural production into the overall centrally planned economy.

Over the last three decades, however, Cuba's agricultural policies have considerably deviated from the Marxist-Leninist pattern followed by other socialist countries. For one-and-a-half decades the collectivization of small peasants was not even a goal of Cuban revolutionary policies. The transformations of private farms into production cooperatives did not start before 1977 and, despite some accelerations in the early 1980s, this process is still not fully completed.

Today, Cuba represents a unique case of a Soviet-type agriculture in that the island's present agrarian system encompasses a number of structural features that are not found in other countries under Marxist-Leninist regimes. The following essay describes the chronological development and considers the ideological background of the peculiarities of Cuban agriculture since the revolution.

Agrarian reform laws and integration plans

The high share of State farms in the total agriculturally utilized and non-utilized area on the one hand, and the high average sizes of both the State and private farms, on the other hand, were results of the two agrarian reform laws of 1959 and 1963, and the following 'integration plans', which were carried out during the period 1967 to 1977. Since the integration plans continued the structural policies established with the agrarian reforms, they are rightly described by Dumont as the 'third' agrarian reform (Dumont, 1974: 64).

The agrarian reform was carried out in two steps: the first Agrarian Reform Law, dated 17 May 1959, stated that all farms over 402 hectares must be nationalized. In special cases, e.g. where the productivity was extraordinarily high or where there was a production specialization, farms up to 1,342 ha (including grazing land), were allowed to continue their operations. Based on these and additional laws, the share of State-owned land increased to 4.4 million ha by May 1961, or 49 per cent of the total land available (agriculturally utilized and non-utilized land); the privately-owned land amounted to 4.6 million ha, or 51 per cent (Gutelman, 1970: 57–61; Acosta, 1972: 93–105).

The agrarian reform converted the sugar cane plantations and cattle farms into so-called sugar co-operatives (Cooperativas Cañeras) and national farms (Granjas del Pueblo), respectively, and put them under the control of the National Institute for Agrarian Reform 'INRA' (Instituto Nacional para Reforma Agraria). But such types of operation had little in common with co-operatives in the real sense of the word: INRA appointed the leading members, determined the type and quality of the production, supplied the operating funds and sold the products. Finally, in 1962, the term 'State farms' came into usage (Mesa-Lago, 1978: 276).

After the first agrarian reform, approximately 11,000 medium- and large-scale farms over 67 ha accounted for about 2.1 million ha, or almost half the privately owned land. Through the second agrarian reform, dated 3 October 1963, which set 67 ha as the new maximum limit for private farms, these were almost completely nationalized with owners' compensation. This land was also transferred to the State sector, increasing the latter's share of the total area (*tierras del país*) to 76 per cent. The state farms' share of the total cultivable land (*tierras cultivables*) was notably lower with 63 per cent (Acosta, 1972: 105–8).[1]

In contrast to the Russian October Revolution of 1917 and the land reforms occurring after 1945 in countries under Soviet control, which distributed most of the land and operating means of large operations to peasants and small land owners, the Cuban agrarian reform did not foresee a distribution of this kind. The agrarian reform declared about 100,000 small farmers as owners and transferred to an additional 100,000 farmer families the land which they had thus far cultivated as tenants, sharecroppers, or even without a valid legal title (so-called *precaristas*); neither of these actions resulted in the creation of new farms (Gómez, 1983: 7–9).[2]

However, the new government under Fidel Castro not only avoided increasing the number of small farms, but also failed to make the small farmers increase the size of their land up to 27 ha, free of charge, or to permit them to purchase additional land up to a maximum of 67 ha, as promised in the first Agrarian Reform Law. Therefore, according to census data, the average farm size in 1965 was only 13 ha, and about half of these were of less than 7 ha (Aranda, 1968: 147, 162). Thus, the rhetorical goal of the agrarian reform, i.e. to overcome the *minifundium* through increasing the farm sizes, was not achieved. However, at least the operations up to 67 ha remained intact so that the farms in Cuba were larger than the average in Poland or Yugoslavia.

Even after the agrarian reform was officially completed in 1965, the revolutionary government strove to transform the private farms into state-owned operations.

First, they limited the rights of owners by prohibiting the lease or sale of property. The laws gave the State the first right of purchase if a farm was given up, and stipulated that in the case of an owner's death, the heirs would be entitled to their inheritance only if they continued to operate the farm. Otherwise, the property would be transferred to the State (RCJ, 1977: 72–96; Alvarez, 1981: 91–3).

Second, starting in 1967, the attempt was made to establish so-called integration plans. The intention of these plans was for the State to purchase farms from small landowners. Normally, these farmers continued to operate their former farm as State farm workers according to a central plan. Moreover, an attempt was made to increase the governmental influence on the farms' production through 'specialization' and 'management plans'. In this case, the farmer was obliged to follow the production plan of a state farm, but remained owner of his farm; he was forced to specialize in certain products, mainly sugar cane, citrus fruits and tobacco, and received operating funds and services from the government. The success, however, was only minimal. After one decade (1977), only 30,000 farmers, 15 per cent of all farmer families, had agreed to take part in an integration or specialization plan (Gey, 1984a: 236–8).

In 1977, at the Fifth Congress of the National Association of Small-Scale Farmers (Asociación Nacional de Agriculturos Pequeños – ANAP), the concept of integration plans was finally discarded. This plan, as Fidel Castro explained to the delegates, would consume huge investment sums in order to convince the farmers (mostly living in scattered settlements) of the advantages of an integration by establishing new villages, complete with modern apartments, electricity and water, schools and clinics, as well as other social benefits. Moreover, it would take about thirty more years to integrate the remaining 1.5 million ha land of the individual farmers; the country could not wait that long (Castro, 1979: 343–9). Until that time, the government had increased the share of State-owned property to approximately 80 per cent through sanctions and integration plans.

The brigade system on State farms

In 1981, 419 state farms comprised about 7.9 million ha (see Table 4.1). With an average size of around 18,900 ha, the Cuban State farms were about as large as those in Bulgaria (18,800 ha), they clearly exceeded the Soviet 'sovchozes' (16,500 ha) and were much larger than the State farms in Poland (2,800 ha) or in Hungary (3,700 ha) (Gey and Wädekin, 1986: 23).

Cuban officials informed the author in 1985 that, up until 1981, the state farms were organized exclusively into 'process-oriented' brigades. 'Process-oriented' meant that each brigade carried out only one particular activity, such as ploughing, watering, maintenance, construction, etc. Since 1981, these brigades have been gradually replaced by so-called integral brigades (*brigadas integrales*). The new brigades cover the various production areas which are involved in the manufacturing of a certain product. They are provided with their own production means and wage funds and are expected to independently fulfil the production tasks assigned to them, i.e. based on their own production plan and with their own profit and loss statement (*cálculo económico interno*) (*Trabajadores*, 25 November 1985: 4; *Granma Resumen Semanal*, 9 February 1986: 4).

It is planned gradually to introduce this new type of brigade into various economic sectors. However, due to the relatively simple production processes in agriculture, this sector is serving as a forerunner. In 1981, the Ministry of Agriculture was the first State agency to organize nineteen integral brigades on nine State farms with a total of 3,020 workers. These brigades are also called 'new type brigades' (*brigadas del nuevo tipo*) or 'permanent brigades' (*brigadas permanentes*). In May 1986, the number of brigades totalled 2,055 and more than 50 per cent existed in the agricultural sector.

In 1985, the average number of workers per brigade (total economy) amounted to fifty nine. The minimum number of workers per brigades is set at fifty, the maximum at eighty, including both blue- and white-collar workers. If an enterprise has more than fifteeen brigades, they are required to establish an intermediary level formed by 'production units' (*unidades de producción*) (Gey, 1987a: Chapter III).

In principle, the brigade members are to be paid according to the team's contribution to the total profit of the enterprise. But in 1984, the Ministry of the Sugar Industry (MINAZ) reported that out of 144 'agro-industrial complexes', only 66 were profitable (*Trabajadores*, 12 September 1985: 1). Hence, on state farms which are running at a loss, wages and bonuses are still linked to labour norms, as it was the case under the former brigade system.

The Cuban Labour Confederation reported that the new brigade system is still suffering from many deficiencies with regard to planning and control, incentives and organization. The labour headquarters pointed out that the most significant problems were not caused by the brigades but by the original 'System of Economic Management and Planning' itself (*Trabajadores*, 16 May 1986: 4). For example, the bonus system existing in Cuba's planning system is so complicated and inefficient that in the Guantánamo province, bonuses for the 1981 coffee harvest could not be paid before 1985 when half of the former pickers had already moved away (*Trabajadores*, 8 April 1985: 4; *Trabajadores*, 3 December 1985: 5). In other words, the future success of the new brigade system largely depends on an efficient overall economic system.

Collectivization of small land owners

While in Poland in 1981, private farms were declared to be unassailable, and in the early 1980s, the Chinese government dissolved the People's Communes to the advantage of private farming, the agrarian Cuban policy took an orthodox turn. In December 1975, the First Congress of the Communist Party of Cuba passed a resolution 'on the agrarian situation and the relationship to farmers', according to which 'all types' of private property should be vanquished and a 'uniform economic system with solely public forms of ownership of production means' be created:

> In the coming years it is necessary to advance to higher forms of production in the farming sector until a complete transformation and integration into the socialist sector of our economy is achieved. (Resolución. . ., 1976: 163–65)

Individual farms which were surrounded by State farms were to be 'integrated' into these as was previously done.

The majority of the farmers, however, were expected, with governmental support, voluntarily to join together to form 'production co-operatives' (Cooperativas de Producción Agropecuaria).

Up until this point, the government had limited itself to grouping the farmers into 'farm associations' (Asociaciones Campesinas) and 'loan and service co-operatives' (Cooperativas de Crédito y Servicios). Both organizations, which are reminiscent of the 'Association of Mutual

Farmer Aid' in East Germany and Eastern Europe, were intended not only to simplify the distribution of inputs and disbursement of loans, but also to guarantee the ideological-political influence on the farmer households. Rather, the government also wanted to counteract the farmers' suspicion that a further agrarian reform was planned which could have only meant a nationalization or collectivization of the small-scale farms.

But again, in contrast to the communist countries in Eastern Europe and Asia, where agrarian reforms were shortly followed by collectivization campaigns, in Cuba, initially no production co-operatives were created. In 1963, the land of the so-called Agricultural Associations (Sociedades Agropecuarias), which are seen in Cuba today as the predecessors of the production co-operatives, made up only 37,000 ha or 0.4 per cent of the total. Frequently, these were not composed of farmers but rather of workers who received land and operating funds from the government. They did not experience any particular governmental support, however, and out of the agricultural associations, only 44 survived in the second half of the 1970s (Gey, 1984b: 210: *Bosquejo histórico*, 1985: 34–5).

A few months before the collectivization decision was reached by the First Party Congress, the president of the small landowners association, José Ramírez, warned against engaging in collectivization as a random campaign. The point was not that a few enthusiastic cadre joined together their property. It affected farmers' land, on which the grandparents of the present owners had already lived. Therefore, Ramírez demanded a 'responsible and thorough preparation' (Ramírez, 1975: 28). When five years later, the Second Party Congress (December 1980) drew a balance, according to official data, only 12 per cent of the non-state property (without plots) was attributed to the production co-operatives (Leiva, 1983: 27). From 1981 to 1983, the collectivization process was then significantly accelerated. The national management of the ANAP committed itself to retaining the exceeding the yearly collectivization quota and added that problems, which arose due to lack of funds, should not hinder the formation of production co-operatives (Gey, 1984: 212–13). Until the beginning of 1984, the share of production co-operatives on non-state owned property rose to 56 per cent (Ramírez, in *Granma*, 24 February 1984).

In 1983, two laws came into effect which were intended to increase the number of production cooperative members: On January 18, the State Council issued a decree giving production co-operative members and their families significant social benefits (*Granma*, 5 April 1983), while farmer families were still denied any financial assistance in the case of pregnancy, infirmity or death. Moreover, with the help of an old-age pension, older farmers were given a strong incentive to join a production co-operative in order to receive this retirement benefit (ANAP, 1985, 1, 22–3).

A further law, dated 1 April 1983, stipulated that private producers were required to pay the State a tax of 5 per cent on their gross profits. If, at the end of a given year, a gross profit over 3,000 pesos remained after taxation, then this was subject to additional progressive taxation of up to 20 per cent. On the other hand, for production co-operative members the net profit was used as the basis for calculating their income tax (ANAP, 1983, 6: 27). One year later, the State finance committee decided that the progressive taxation of gross profit 'de-motivated' the small landowners and passed an amendment on 13 July 1984, stipulating a general 5 per cent tax on the gross profit of private producers. Moreover, all producers supplying products intended for export such as coffee, cocoa or tobacco, were exempt from this tax liability (ANAP, 1984, 9: 16).

In February 1986, Fidel Castro stated that the production co-operatives accounted for an area of 1,072,055 ha and their share in the total non-state-owned land was 61.3 per cent (Castro, 1986a: 12). This means that the collectivization process in 1984 and 1985 again drastically decelerated, compared to the period 1981–3. Already in May 1984, the ANAP president Ramírez stated in an interview with the magazine *Bohemia*, that one is neither in a hurry with the collectivization, nor does one want 'confused' members (ANAP 1984, 8: 18). One year later he added that the areas of the production co-operatives could not be expanded by continuing to let the previous owners retire. In the future, more time must be devoted to the 'control and management' of the process (ANAP 1985, 7: 14).

At least two reasons could have caused the State and party leadership to stop the collectivization process: the high costs of social benefits, of equipping the production co-operatives and developing infrastructure, as well as the numerous problems of the co-operative operational management. The collectivization also required extraordinary investments in vehicles and machines because the farmers possessed mainly animal-driven vehicles due to the mechanization prohibition, and therefore contributed only a few outdated tractors and trucks (Gey, 1984b: 212).

Since the traditional farms in Cuba were generally scattered, extensive investments were also required to establish complete settlements and villages near to the production co-operatives. Up until April 1985, the national bank had financed 10,000 apartments; an additional 10,000 were built by the members out of their own funds with the support of the regional administrations. One of the unavoidable infrastructure measures was to supply electricity and water; at the above-mentioned time, only 740, or somewhat over the half of all production co-operatives had been supplied with electricity (ANAP, 1985, 8: 21–2).

The manner in which the farmers have recently been forced to integrate their operations into production co-operatives is reminiscent of the integration plans covering the years 1967–77, when the political leadership also tried to buy the farmers' independence. In October 1985, a Cuban official stated at a meeting with German visitors, among them the present writer, that the costs of establishing the production co-operatives could possibly not be 'recovered' even in 'a hundred years'. In many cases, it was admitted, the advantages of a large-scale production are 'initially more potential than actual'; and on the whole one must appeal to the 'consciousness'. Thus, many co-operative chairmen probably experience situations similar to the one who reported that from the three million litres of fuel his co-operative needed to produce the planned quantity of rice, only 700,000 litres were actually received (ANAP, 1985, 7: 13). That this was not an isolated case was evidenced by the appeal of the ANAP president, namely not to use tractors when teams of oxen are standing around (ANAP, 1985, 12: 11).

Individual and collective plots

Until the beginning of the 1980s, there was little dependable information on Cuban plot farming. On the one hand, it was considered certain that approximately 290,000 State farm workers were allowed to farm plots for their own consumption only up to 1967; however, they were not allowed to sell surpluses nor to keep livestock (Bernardo, 1971: 193). On the other hand, the Cuban Statistical Yearbook 1974, listed the plots of former farmers, workers and other private persons (Anuario, 1974: 46–9). This information was basically confirmed by an additional publication of the Statistical Committee of 1981 (*Cuba*, 1981: 63). The Cuban authors V. Figueroa and L.A. García used this as a basis for a

Table 4.1 Types and sizes of farms according to sectors, 1974 and 1981

Type	Number	Area 1,000 ha[a]		Average in ha[b]	Share of total Area (%)	
	1981	1974	1981	1981	1974	1981
1. State farms	419	8,918	7,921	18,904.3	79.8	80.8
2. Production co-operatives	1,118	6	384[c]	342.7	0.1	4.0
3. Private farms	98,113	1,993	1,247	12.7	17.9	12.7
4. Plots of former farmers,	16,279	n.a.	31	1.9	0.3	0.3
of workers, etc.	47,741[d]	213	216	4.5	1.9	2.2
Total	163,670	11,167	9,799	—	100.2	100.0

Notes: (a) Total area
   (b) Author's calculation
   (c) Including 64,000 ha state-owned land turned over for utilization.
   (d) Including non-farmer owners with more than 67 ha
Source: Anuario, 1974: 48/9; Figueroa Arbelo and García de la Torre, 1984: 39

table they published in 1984 which, for the first time, listed all agricultural producer categories.

In the category 'plots' it is somewhat surprising that in addition to the 47,741 workers, pensioners and other plot owners, also non-farmers owners are included with more than 67 ha, without indicating what type of owners these are. It is puzzling as to why they have been included under the category of plot owners. The average plot farm size of 4.5 ha would then equal that of a small-scale farm. In the accompanying text, Figueroa Arbela and García de la Torre (1984: 43) explain that the 'wide majority' of plots range between 0.44 and 0.86 ha. This somewhat exceeds the average known size in East Europe.

Figueroa and García differentiate between the peasant farm representing only a traditional form which will eventually disappear, and the plot farm (1984: 58–9). In conformity with the 'line' valid in the USSR since 1965, they declared the latter to be a form of personal property within the socialist system which, due to their production reserves, represents an 'objective necessity'. This opinion is in direct contrast to statements made by Fidel Castro at the Sixth ANAP congress in 1982, where the *máximo líder* stated that through the collectivization, the private producers within the Cuban agriculture would simply disappear. In the future, there would be only a collective use of the plots for self-consumption by workers and co-operative members in the State farms and production co-operatives. He added that one did not exactly know who owned land legally or illegally. Ten thousands of ha existed which were registered neither by the Ministry of Agriculture nor by the Small Land Owners Association (*Bohemia*, 28 May 1982: 76 and 74).

But the advocates of the individual plot farms in line with the Soviet model could not come up against the followers of the collective self-sufficiency system on state farms and production co-operatives. Under the title 'Adiós al conuco' (farewell to the plots), the magazine *Bohemia* reported on the abolition of the individual plots and the expansion of the collective self-sufficiency system on State farms. For example, in the future, the agricultural-industrial complexes of the sugar sector should provide food-stuffs for 1.3 million people (13 per cent of the population), using land intended for self-sufficiency farming. As far as possible, these farm sections should be supplied with the necessary equipment and other means normally not available in this economic sector but which are needed for the rice harvest or for feeding cattle (*Bohemia*, 4 October 1985: 28–31). As on State farms, a special brigade is devoted to collective self-sufficiency farming in the production co-operatives.

So far, there is no general statistical information on the average size of the farm sections worked collectively for self-consumption. In two cases, it comprised about two to three per cent of the land; whereby either 0.2 or 0.7 ha was allocated to each co-operative member (ANAP, 1985, 2: 12; author's own researches in October 1985). In collective self-sufficiency farming, one such section cultivates various plant crops, with the exception of industrial raw materials; in the area of animal production both poultry and small animals are raised, as well as cattle, pigs and sheep. The products are sold to the members over co-operative-run 'agricultural markets' (Agromercado). As long as the free peasant markets existed, the production co-operatives and State farms were obliged to sell their surpluses from self-sufficiency farming exclusively to the state (ANAP, 1985, 2: 21, 30; ANAP 1985, 4: 12; ANAP 1985, 5: 7,11).

State and non-State agricultural commercialization

As was previously the case in Eastern Europe, in 1959 Cuba began to establish State organizations for the purchasing of agricultural products. Since 1962, under the term 'Acopio', there have been national purchasing organizations which buy certain products at fixed prices from both State and private farms.

Traditionally, peasant farming in Cuba was highly specialized and thus strongly geared towards a commercialization of the products. The small landowners made between 70 and 80 per cent of their income with sugar cane, tobacco and coffee. Since 1961, the entire amount or majority of these products must be sold to Acopio or directly to the respective national industrial establishment (Figueroa Arbelo and García de la Torre, 1984: 38–40).

Otherwise, the farmers preferred to sell a significant proportion of their food products (according to estimates, from one to three-quarters) to consumers and middlemen. These direct sales were not illegal and were even transacted by ANAP functionaries and loan and service co-operatives. The purchasers were by no means only private parties, but also national institutions, such as the armed forces, the tourist bureau or canteens of State-owned companies. According to a government study, the private retailers (about half of which were 'pedlars' of groceries and beverages) purchased around two-thirds of their goods via private channels or directly from farmers (Domínguez, 1978: 451–5; Ayala, 1982: 18).

In spring 1968, the government nationalized the remaining private business in a 'revolutionary offensive', and in December 1971, the Fourth ANAP Congress declared private sales by farmers to be illegal. Although since then agricultural products up to no more than 25 pounds could be sent to relatives in other areas, the authorities could not stop large quantities of goods from reaching the cities via illegal channels. Only towards the end of the 1970s did the government give up its fight against the black market through raids and street blockades and tolerated farmers selling their products at freely bargained prices (Handelman 1981/2: 140).

Finally, on 3 April 1980, the Executive Committee of the Council of Ministers announced the readmission of 'free peasant markets'. The decree stipulated that both individial farmers and plot owners, as well as production co-operatives and loan and service co-operatives and co-operative members and State farm workers (however not the State farm itself) could sell produce from their surplus and by-production directly to consumers at free prices. 'Surplus' was termed to be the produce remaining after the farmers delivered the contractual quantity to the State; 'by-products' were all non-contractual produce. Cattle and beef, tobacco, coffee and cocoa were generally excluded from the peasant markets because one wanted to avoid a decrease in the national cattle supply as well as in the delivery quantities of important export products (Gey, 1984a: 247–8).

However, the success of the free commercialization of agricultural produce soon came up against the ideological bias of the State and party leadership. It is true that in December 1980, the Second Congress of the Communist party explicitly welcomed the creation of free peasant markets and requested the government agencies to grant them the neccessary support (ANAP, 1981, 2). However, due to the continued high price level and the considerable profit made by some sellers, the party ideologists saw their fears confirmed that free markets would encourage a private capital accumulation.

Castro, as the chief of State and party, was one of the leading opponents of the pragmatic course. In two speeches in the spring of 1982, he raged against the 'shadowy figures' causing 'chaos' and 'disorder' at the peasant markets. He defined the peasant markets as a 'capitalistic formula' which must be applied until the 'selfish and uneconomical *minifundium*' disappears in complicance with the collectivization. Castro admitted, however, that the insufficient production of the State farms as well as the numerous shortcomings within the Acopio system caused the large demand on the free markets (Castro, 1982a; 1982b).

For their part, the co-operative members and individual farmers criticized the inflexibility and imbalance of the State producer prices which offered neither a production incentive nor a reasonable income. The organizational services of the national purchasing network were also criticized due to 'subjective and objective deficiencies' (ANAP, 1984, 4: 19; 1984, 11: 18; 1984, 12: 12–14; 1985, 7: 10–13). Despite the pressure on private producers and production co-operatives not to sell their surpluses at free markets, but instead to the State, the peasant markets still retained their attraction.

While in 1982, the economic ramifications of a renewed repression of the free markets were evidently still under consideration, the party and State leadership, in 1986, finally decided to forbid the peasant markets due to 'pressure' from the production co-operative chairmen. At the Second National Meeting of the production Co-operatives (17/18 May 1986), in which nearly all politburo and government members participated, Castro announced that one would fight all types of 'parasitism' and 'neo-capitalism' which had appeared at peasant markets and in other economic sectors. The remaining farmers, he maintained, had made such large profits at the free markets that they had absolutely no incentive to join a production co-operative. In the past, one had been too generous with 'certain elements' within society who retreated from farming and chose to lease their land. The misuse of property by a few 'kulaks' would now be punished with dispossession (*Trabajadores*, 21 May 1986).

Castro described the gap in supplies caused by the prohibition of the free markets as insignificant. The annual turnover of the peasant markets amounted to only about 70 million pesos. Compared to the food sales of State-owned retailers in 1984, this would give the free peasant markets a share of about 2.2 per cent (calculated according to Anuario, 1984: 263).

In order to replace the produce supplied by the free pesant markets, it was intended to improve the national buying system 'Acopio' and to expand the 'national parallel markets' (Mercados Paralelos Estatales). These markets usually offer rationed or insufficiently available products at prices significantly higher than in the normal national retail stores, as well as high quality consumer goods and imported products. In the future, these stores should offer a larger assortment of agricultural products.

Between 'revolutionary offensive' and Soviet-orientated pragmatism

The goals and measures of the post-revolutionary agrarian policies in Cuba were always subject to the leading political-ideological models. These, however, were neither constant nor undisputed. Between 1963 and 1965, two positions emerged for the first time in the so-called socialism debate, both parties of which were represented by influential members of the political leaderships: a moralistic-leftist and a Soviet-pragmatic position. Both viewpoints, which are again currently in debate, contain partly corresponding and partly contradictory conclusions on the agrarian policy.

In the socialism debate, Che Guevara led the one group (starting in 1963); he demanded that the money and commodity economy be abolished, that the companies be managed as a single factory and that a 'new man' be summoned who would be dedicated to the revolution and free from self-interest. Carlos Rafael Rodríguez and other former members of the Socialist People's party formed the second group; they fought for a reform of the planning and management system similar to that which was started in the Soviet Union. The Soviet-orientated pragmatist suggested, among other things, decentralizing the decision-making rights of the companies and utilizing the 'commodity-money-relationships'.

The defeat of the pragmatists allowed a mobilization regime to take over in Cuba during the years 1966 to 1970, which was reminiscent of the Cultural Revolution occurring at the same time in China. During the 'sinoguevaristic' phase (Mesa-Lago, 1978: 1–10), both the plots of State farm workers, as well as the remaining private operations were disposed of, mainly in the retail and service sectors, and the attempt was made to integrate the remaining family-run farms into the national sector through integration plans. As a result, particularly the supply quantities from the private agricultural sector dropped dramatically. Cuban authors attest to this:

> The procurement quantities for roots and tubers, grains and vegetables decreased by about 46 per cent in 1970, from almost 70 million pesos to 37.7 million pesos. While in 1967 the small landowners provided 65.6 per cent of the nationwide supply of grain, roots and tubers as well as vegetables, their contribution in 1970 sank to 23.6 per cent. (*Bosquejo histórico*, 1985: 48).

At the beginning of the 1970s, as previously from 1961 to 1965, a transformation of the economy took place, which conformed to the Soviet model. The government limited the mass mobilization activities and other 'voluntary', unpaid use of labour, reduced the pressure on farmers to agree with integration plans (i.e. give up their farms) and raised the producer prices. The private producers reacted positively to the modified agrarian policy. The farmers not only supplied larger quantities to the national buying organization Acopio, but also intensified the farming of their land. Cuban authors mention that in spite of the private area planted being much smaller in 1976 than in 1972, the output of roots and tubers increased by 50 per cent during this time and that of vegetables by 81 per cent (Figueroa Arbelo and García de la Torre, 1984: 38).

In December 1975, the First Congress of the Communist party announced the introduction of the 'System of Economic Planning and Management'. The delegates thus spoke out for a decentralized Soviet-type planning model and agreed that monetary categories should be used only sparingly. However, the simultaneous decision to collectivize the remaining private farms also showed a basic agreemeent between the moralistic-leftists following Fidel Castro and the Soviet-orientated pragmatists following Carlos Rafael Rodríguez: neither party wing allowed the small landowner any possibilities for development in Cuba's otherwise completely nationalized economy.

The two groups had different opinions on other agrarian policy matters: the introduction of free peasant markets in the spring of 1980 and suggestions on how the individual plots of State farm workers and production co-operative members, and also of other garden owners, could be used to supply the population with food (Figueroa Arbelo and García de la Torre, 1984) emphasize the strong position of the pragmatists in the first half of the 1980s. Although this underlines the great success of the free peasant markets, their long-term expectations were still aimed at replacing the free marketing of agricultural surpluses with parastatal consumer co-operatives.

Since the end of 1984, the Soviet-orientated functionaries and technocrats quickly lost their influence.[3] Their intentions never went as far as the goals of the 'Prague Spring' or the economic reforms in Hungary and China. In the context of the reforms of other socialist systems in the 1980s, they actually appear as 'hard-liners'. But they are the ones who support the decentralization of decision making, simplification of planning methods, financial autonomy of companies, as well as individual plots within the State farms and production co-operatives. In this, they could refer to no less than the General Secretary of the Communist Party of the Soviet Union, Mikhail Gorbachev.

Whether in the near future Cuba will utilize the reform atmosphere set by Moscow is more than questionable. By mid-1986, Castro started a 'revolutionary counter-offensive' against 'neo-capitalists', 'exposed capitalists', 'scoundrels' and 'usurers' which, similar to that of 1968, is characterized by moralism and puritanism. At the Third Congress of the Communist Party, Castro showed his disappointment and obvious disgust with the behaviour of workers and small landowners, managers and chairmen of production co-operatives, as well as of leading party and administrative cadres, under the conditions of the new 'System of Economic Management and Planning (SEMP)'. They had all made personal profits at the cost of the public. Above all, he was outraged by the fact that State farms and production co-operatives exchanged products and services among themselves, thus depriving the population. Castro appealed to the consciousness and selflessness of the revolutionaries. Politics should always control the economy, and the economic mechanisms should only be 'tools of the political and revolutionary activities' (Castro, 1986b: 3–4).

Castro's lapse back into the leftist radicalism of the 1960s is basically an expression of his disappointment with the new planning and management system. After more than a decade, the SEMP has still not been fully introduced and, up until now, has proven to be extremely cumbersome and bureaucratic (Gey, 1987a). At the same time, Castro's anti-market and anti-money ideology hinders any decentraliztion and flexibilization of the economy.

One of the first victims of the 'revolutionary counter-offensive' were the free peasants markets. They were forbidden in May 1986. In order to prevent supply deficiencies, functionaries of the national buying organization Acopio inspected the fields of the private farms and controlled the planting of summer crops (*Trabajadores*, 26 May 1986: 1). In general, the authorities were optimistic that the cities would receive sufficient food supplies (*Trabajadores*, 23 May 1986: 1). Towards the end of the year, the supply problems worsened, and in November, the Ministry of Agriculture admitted that the food assortment offered left something to be desired. Obviously, according to a Western news correspondent, the prohibition of the free peasant markets was affecting the supply of food to the cities (García, 1986: 2).

Of course, the importance of the free peasant markets in overall Cuban economic activities was minimal. Their recent illegalization has indicated however, that Castro is presently not willing to take a more pragmatic approach to solving the island's urgent economic problems.

Notes

This chapter is based on my article 'Kubanische Agrarpolitik zwischen Sowjetmodell und Castros Utopie', *Osteuropa, Zeitschrift für Gegenwartsfragen des Ostens*, 37 (1987), 1: 42–56.

1. These figures are from census data and do not represent all of the areas covered by the agrarian reform. A contemporary Cuban source lists the total area in 1981 at about 9.8 million hectares, which is around 800,000 hectares larger than in census figures from two decades earlier, May 1961 (Figueroa Arbelo and García de la Torre, 1984: 39).
2. A Cuban authors' collective summarizes the result of the agrarian reform as follows: 'The agrarian reform led to a rapid increase in one form of leasing relationship or another, but did not create any new farmers' (*Bosquejo histórico*, 1985: 22).
3. Clear signs of the defeat of the pragmatists were the dismissal of Humberto Pérez as chairman of the National Planning Commission JUCEPLAN, and as vice president of the council of ministers in the middle of 1985, and the establishment of a 'National Committee of Economic Management' in May 1986. This commission took over the basic duties of JUCEPLAN and became directly subordinate to the executive board of the council of ministers (chairman: Fidel Castro). (For more details, see Gey, 1987b; Pérez-López, 1986).

References

Acosta, J. (1972) 'Las leyes de reforma agraria en Cuba y el sector privado campesino', *Economía y Desarrollo*, 12: 93–105.

Alvarez, F. (1981) *Comentarios a la Constitución Socialista*, La Habana.

ANAP (Official Organ of the National Association of Small Peasants, monthly), La Habana.

Anuario Estadístico de Cuba (1974, 1975, 1984) Comité Estatal de
Estadísticas (ed.), La Habana (various issues).

Aranda, S. (1968) *La revolución agraria en Cuba*, México.

Ayala, H., (1982) 'Transformación de propiedad en el período 1964–1980',
Economía y Desarrollo. **68**: 10–25.

Bernardo, R.M. (1971) 'Managing and Financing the Farm', in
Revolutionary Change in Cuba C. Mesa-Lago (ed.), Pittsburgh:
185–208.

Bosquejo histórico de cooperación socialista de la agricultura cubana
(various authors), La Habana, 1985.

Castro, F. (1979) 'En la clausura del V. Congreso de la ANAP', in F.
Castro, *Discursos*, Vol. III, La Habana: 337–71.

Castro, F. (1982a) 'Discurso al VI. Congreso de la ANAP', *Bohemia*, 22,
28 May: 68–79.

Castro, F. (1982b) 'Discurso en el acto de la clausura del IV. Congreso de
la Unión de Jóvenes Comunistas', *Carribbean Monthly Bulletin* (Institute
of Carribbean Studies, Puerto Rico) 4: 4–9.

Castro, F. (1986a) 'Informe Central al Tercer Congreso' *Granma*. Resumen
Semanal, 16 February.

Castro, F. (1986b) 'Discurso en la clausura de la sesión diferida del Tercer
Congreso del Partido, el día 2 de diciembre de 1986', *Trabajadores*, 8
December.

Chonchol, J. (1963) 'Análisis crítico de la reforma agraria cubana', *El
Trimestre Económico*, **117**, México.

Cuba. Desarrollo económico y social durante el período 1958-1980 (1981),
Comité Estatal de Estadísticas (ed.), La Habana.

Domínguez, J.I. (1978) *Cuba. Order and Revolution*, Cambridge, London.

Dumont, R. (1974) *Is Cuba Socialist?*, New York.

Figueroa Arbelo, V., García de la Torre, L.A. (1984) 'Apuntes sobre
la comercialización agrícola no estatal', *Economía y Desarrollo* **83**:
34–61.

García, J. (1986) *La economía cubana enfrenta uno de sus momentos más
difíciles*, International Press Service, 23 December.

Gey, P. (1984a) 'Die Stellung des privaten Agrarsektors in der kubanischen
Wirtschaft', in Th. Bergmann, P. Gey, W. Quaisser, (eds),
Sozialistische Agrarpolitik, Köln: 232–57.

Gey, P. (1984b) 'Die Kollektivierung der kleinbäuerlichen Landwirtschaft
in Kuba', *Agrarwirtschaft*, **33**, 7: 209–16.

Gey, P. (1987a) 'The Cuban economy under the new "system of
management and planning". Success or failure?', in P. Gey, J. Kosta,
W. Quaisser, (eds), *Crisis and Reform in Socialist Economies*,
Boulder/Colorado: 71–98.

Gey, P. (1987b) 'L'économie cubaine entre réforme et "contre-offensive
révolutionnaire"', *Le Courrier des Pays de l'Est*, **323**: 6–13.

Gey, P., Wädekin, K.-E. (1986) 'Agrarpolitik', *Pipers Wörterbuch zur
Politik. Sozialistische Systeme*, **4**: 19–29.

Gómez, O. (1983) *De la finca individual a la cooperativa agropecuaria*, La
Habana.

Granma and *Granma. Resumen Semanal* (Official Organ of the Central Committee of the Communist Party of Cuba), La Habana.

Gutelman, M. (1970) *La agricultura socializada en Cuba*, México.

Handelman, H. (1981/2) 'Cuban Food Policy and Popular Nutritional Levels', *Cuban Studies*, **2** (1981) and **1** (1982): 127–46.

Leiva, Ch. (1983) 'La ANAP le ha dado un apoyo valiosísimo al Partido', *ANAP*, 3: 26–7.

Mesa-Lago, C. (1978) *Cuba in the 1970s, Pragmatism and Institutionalisation*, Albuquerque.

Pérez-López, J. (1986) 'Cuban Economy in the 1980s', *Problems of Communism*, **35**, 5: 16–34.

Ramírez, J. (1975) 'Palabras en la sesión de clausura del Pleno Nacional de la ANAP', *ANAP*, 5: 26–33.

RCJ (1977) 'El Nuevo Derecho Agrario en Cuba', *Revista de Ciencias Jurídicas*, San José/Costa Rica: 72–96.

'Resolución sobre la cuestión agraria y las relaciones con el campesinado', *Economía y Desarrollo*, 1976, **36**: 160–7.

Trabajadores (Central Organ of the Cuban Labour Confederation, daily), La Habana.

Chapter five

Vietnamese agriculture – changing property rights in a mature collectivized agriculture

Adam Fforde[1]

Introduction

This chapter deals with various aspects of the system of agricultural organization adopted in communist Vietnam. This system has changed over time, and has posed a number of distinct problems to the foreign analyst. The basic model – the collective farm – is derived from Soviet experience, but has been greatly modified. For this there are many reasons, perhaps the most important of which are: first, the extremely low level of socio-economic development in Vietnam prior to the Revolution; second, the quite different technical conditions of production involved in rice cultivation (see Fforde, 1988) compared with those in the Soviet Union; third, the important cultural and historical legacies with which the Vietnamese confronted the various difficulties posed by collectivization in particular and the construction of socialism in general; fourth, the extended period of war that lasted intermittently from the Declaration of Independence in 1945 to national reunification in 1975. Since then, violence has continued intermittently as a result of international tensions surrounding the Cambodia question, and since 1979 the Vietnamese military presence in that country. The period of open warfare with China during 1979 was followed by intermittent armed conflicts on the Sino-Vietnamese border.

In a similar way to other developing countries that have adopted Marxism-Leninism, Vietnam, therefore, can be expected to contribute to our understanding of comparative social development.

Research into modern Vietnam lags way behind that regarding many other developing countries.[2] One result of this seems to be an excessive tendency towards theoretical concerns as inadequate data confronts a natural interest in answering major questions. However, in an institutional environment that remains unfamiliar to most readers, clear definitions are needed for exposition of research results. The complex realities of property rights in modern Vietnamese rural society are far from being well understood. Furthermore, it is likely that the analysis of collectivized Vietnamese agriculture poses theoretical questions that require at least some modification of the existing theoretical 'tool-kit'. This should cope with three interrelated areas: first, the meaning of 'institutional endogeneity' – the possibility and nature of grass-roots adaptation of developmental models; second, the role in this process of an economic environment where the familiar mechanisms of the central planning model co-exist with extensive unplanned economic relations; third, the analysis in these and other processes of the role of collectives (whether based upon kin groups – 'families' – or not – 'villages') in taking rational economic decisions under conditions combining great uncertainty with the possibility of coercion, which make it practically impossible to quantify the expected outcomes of group strategies.

Most classic analyses of the Soviet model assumed that institutional change is an entirely top-down process. The system is that of a 'strong state' and change must therefore be 'top-down'. When this assumption does not hold, and there are many reasons for supposing that it does not hold in the case of Vietnam, further thought is needed. My own collaborative research has argued strongly that the Democratic Republic of (North) Vietnam (the DRV), which was replaced by the Socialist Republic of Vietnam after the end of the war, is best seen as a 'weak state' and largely unable to implement many central directives effectively (Fforde and Paine, 1987). Unfortunately, however, empirical research remains primitive, and this inevitably weakens theoretical work.

This chapter has four parts. In the first and second, various concepts and definitions that are considered appropriate to the analysis of Vietnamese collectivised agriculture are examined. These are closely bound up with the interactions between co-operators' 'private' – or 'own-account' – activities and other activities, for instance work carried out directly for the co-operative. This is above all intended to bring out the importance of considering what establishes in practice the distinction between 'private', 'collective' and other categories. An important aspect of this discussion is the stress upon the distinction between formal, legally-recognized, property rights and informal property rights enforced by some other system of norms, typically local and customary. In a 'weak state', the struggle to impose a centrally-defined model takes the form of the attempt to enforce formal property rights through the State's legal framework and in other ways. As a matter of definition, throughout this chapter the term 'formal' refers to systems laid down by the politico-administrative centre of the nation-state structure; it is therefore almost synonymous with a limited definition of 'legal'.

The third part of the chapter looks at north Vietnamese experiences with the introduction in agricultural co-operatives of the system known as 'output contracting' and the circumstances of the introduction of this policy. (For a time-table of the collectivizing policies 'from above' in Vietnam, see the introductory chapter of the present volume.) Questions thrown up in this part of the discussion throw light upon the theoretical difficulties mentioned above.

The final part of the chapter introduces a rapid overview of the deep structural difficulties facing the north Vietnamese economy, and the role played by agricultural stagnation within that overall picture. Here it is important to distinguish between the conditions of over-population and climatic uncertainty facing the population in the north and centre of the country from those of relative land abundance and stable weather enjoyed in the Mekong delta of the south. There are easily understood historical reasons for this regional imbalance, for the Vietnamese ethnic heartland was originally the northern delta, from which excess population migrated southwards over the centuries in search of land. This is discussed in Fforde and Paine (1987, Chapter 1), and provides an important element of any understanding of modern development issues in north Vietnam. The paper concludes with a brief evaluation of the reforms introduced in the early 1980s.

The meaning of the 'private'–'collective' dichotomy

The importance of the 'private' sector to the operation of collectivized agriculture has long been well-known (Wädekin 1973; 1982: 94–100; Nove, 1977: 122–6; Ellman 1979: 90; Hedlund, 1989; see also chapter 14 of the companion volume). But research has paid rather less attention to the systemic, or socio-structural importance of the activities associated with, and conventionally if sometimes misleadingly taken to be under the control of, the co-operator household. Thus, to take one example, in the analysis of the political economy of collectivized agriculture, little attention has on the whole been paid to the possibility that the interaction between collective and private activities has tended to support traditional and patriarchal relations within the household, supporting the reproduction of hierarchical gender relations throughout rural areas (see White, 1982, for a valuable summary of the question; also Werner, 1984, for some observations on Vietnamese conditions).

Such considerations throw immediate doubt upon the adequacy of such conceptions as 'household', which is often taken as being synonymous with 'private'. Similar worries arise when one probes the meaning of the word 'collective'; use of the term may lead to an under-estimation of the importance of divisions within co-operative structures. The co-operative can then easily be treated as either a unit having well-defined interests, or, more usually in a Marxist-Leninist system, as the passive tool of superior levels. A way into the question is to examine the internal divisions within the collective itself. In the same way, use of the term 'State' allows one to ignore the frequently far from monolithic character of administrative systems.

Whilst this chapter does not address the important questions posed by the use of terms 'family' and 'State', it does draw upon a longer piece of work that examines the effects (primarily economic) of the internal structure of co-operatives in the case of Vietnam (Fforde, 1989). It has therefore been found valuable to re-examine the meaning of such broad categories as 'collective' and 'private'.

Economic analysis has traditionally been concerned with the factors that determine the processes of production, consumption, distribution and exchange in any given group. The valuable simplification permitted by micro-analysis permits us to limit such questions to behaviour within the chosen micro-unit and the effects of the unit's environment upon such behaviour. In the case of a collectivized agriculture, the micro-unit may usefully be referred to as a 'collectivity'. This is understood to mean the combination of all economic and social activities carried out by the collectivized population of a particular group ('village' or 'commune'). This does not necessarily imply that only the members of the local population who have formally joined the co-operative are members of the collectivity. If some people in the area who remain outside it share direct economic interests with them, then such people are arguably members of the collectivity – their interests enter into the relevant economic calculations. It is therefore a far wider concept than the 'co-operative', and so its use immediately focuses concern upon the key sub-systems within the collectivity and the relations between it and its environment. Use of the term raises the question whether the co-operative dominates socio-economic activity; furthermore, examination of interactions between the co-operative and the rest of the collectivity leads to investigation of the varying relationships between different elements of the co-operative form with the co-operative's environment, and therefore to examination of the internal structure of the co-operative.

Here, only the behaviour of a collectivized system under conditions of 'aggravated shortage' is considered. This term, although only applied to date to Vietnam, seems useful for the analysis of certain types of under-developed countries and/or regions (Fforde and Paine, 1987). It refers to a situation where the familiar pattern of simultaneous shortages and slacks created by the central plan coexists with an extensive development of unplanned activities often but not necessarily, aimed at the free market. The coercion that results from the imposition of supply-duties within the central plan's resource allocation system is typically lacking from the allocative relations associated with unplanned activities.[3]

Free markets are intrinsically voluntary at the point of exchange, but are only one type of unplanned activity, along with swaps, favours, barters and other non-monetized transactions. Free market transactions seem familiar and accessible to established techniques. The value of disposing of some economic resource appears clearly, or so it seems, as market price; similar considerations apply to costs. But for many reasons this is misleading; for example, where planned activities and barter coexist with free markets, money and financial assets generally are not the universal store of value. Free market prices are only one measure of value. *Value therefore depends upon context, and is neither clear nor certain.*

An extremely important aspect of the relations between a collectivity and the outside world under such conditions is the coexistence of various distinct types of allocative relations. In this overall structure the 'plan' and the 'free market' are extremes, or ideal types, that in practice do not exist in isolation from each other. They may have strong mutual interactions, depending upon the circumstances. It is not obvious *a priori* whether any given interaction has a 'zero-sum' characteristic. This suggests that, as extremes, they may profitably be viewed as helping to define the boundaries between the constituent sub-systems of the economic system as a whole. The notion of 'aggravated shortage' is designed to illuminate this.

If this characterization is correct, then neither established market-oriented Western economics nor plan-oriented Soviet conventions apply.[4] Instead, economists and economic agents have to confront an environment where costs and values are extremely important in influencing resource allocation decision, but where there is no clear social indicator of relative costs and values, which vary according to the circumstances of the acquisition and use of resources. This suggests that there is no clear, unambiguous and widely accepted *formal* system of property-rights within such a society, that would generate a clear and pervasively dominant value system.

Research into the operation of collective farms in north Vietnam has strongly suggested that it is the different allocative relations that play a crucial role in explaining the interaction between different sub-systems of the collectivity (Fforde, 1989). Thus, the 'private sector' may be viewed as a spectrum of activities characterized by the relatively voluntary way in which resources are acquired and disposed of, while the 'collective' is dominated by the aspects of compulsion and conditionality that are the corollaries of supply-duties and subsidized deliveries of inputs. While differences in production conditions go a limited way to

111

explaining interactions between these sub-systems, it is the different allocative mechanisms that go far further in explaining their varying performance and their pattern of interaction.

An analysis of the interaction between different allocative systems must investigate the coexistence of different systems of property rights. Naturally, the fact that the questions are easy to put does not mean that they will be easy to answer. These questions cover, at a minimum, the following:

1. The agents involved, both in relation to the object concerned and in the enforcement of that relationship.
2. Rights of access and use.
3. Rights of acquisition and disposal.
4. Interactions between different property-relations, i.e. the possibility of mixed rights, involving more than one agency; and the possibility of conditionality, in that a right is dependent upon recognition of another's right.

Modern nation-states, especially after the creation of Napoleonic law, conventionally seek to establish coherent systems of property rights within a single national legal framework. The agencies involved are simple: the owner is a single legal entity and the enforcer is the legal arm of a sovereign state. Rights of access and use are seen as unlimited in the first instance, constrained only where particular actions would threaten the interests of others. Similar considerations apply to rights of acquisition and disposal. Finally, notions of mixed rights are greatly simplified by the use of corporate bodies, such as trusts and corporations, while the notion of conditionality is quite alien, since rights are presumed unlimited in the first instance. The point is that the meaning of property rights cannot be expected to be static, but will instead be developed in a way appropriate to the nature of a particular group of people.

North Vietnamese agriculture – parameters and agents

A number of factors make north Vietnamese experience of great interest in revealing how the notion of property rights varies under different social conditions. And it is these notions that define in practice what is meant by 'private' and 'collective' in north Vietnamese agriculture. Probably the most striking element of north Vietnamese rural social organization is its strongly collective nature. This is true for both the pre- and post-Revolutionary periods, and has long coexisted with a deep sense of individual and family interests, as well as of the potentially legitimate role of the nation-state (Fforde, 1988). Thus one can talk of Vietnamese culture being simultaneously both highly collective and highly individualistic.

112

There are a number of reasons why collective action should be highly valued by people living under north Vietnamese rural conditions. These have not changed greatly since the Revolution and have largely to do with the high levels of risk and uncertainty.[5]

1. People are poor. Per capita incomes are extremely close to subsistence levels (see Table 5.1). In addition, the weather is unpredictable, so real incomes are risky. (The statistical tables referred to can be found in the Appendix at the end of this chapter.)
2. People are subject to the frequently distant and arbitrary policies of the centre of the nation-state apparatus. Especially since the Revolution, they are used to being uncertain as to whether policy will move in any particular direction, demanding changes in methods of rural social organization.[6]
3. People live in an economic environment dominated by the ever-present existence of chronic shortage. Supplies of needed resources through the state plan reflect the end result of complicated processes of rationed allocations and the other dislocations typical of 'shortage economies' (Kornai, 1980). Not only are the quantity and timing of deliveries both risky and uncertain, but the quality of goods is also unreliable. By limiting information flows, chronic shortage raises the riskiness and uncertainty of the economic environment, encouraging adaptive strategies.
4. The existence of a collectively structured society reinforces, and therefore helps reproduce, collective structures. This is as true for families as it is for producer co-operatives. The cultural basis of the society, which is responsible for generating appropriate belief systems, must exert pressure for the reproduction and support of its own key institutions. Whether they need to or not, people tend to believe in the rationality of what they do. Thus north Vietnamese peasants, who have been collectively taxed for generations (both under the dynasties and since the revolution), naturally see a group interest in uniting to avoid excess taxes. Similarly, any collective institution that possesses its own resources – such as communal land in traditional society – creates incentives for individuals and families to manoeuvre relative to it.

Collectives, however, can be of many types and have many meanings. Furthermore, just as the collective plays a major role in securing various economic and cultural ends, so do the family and other social groups beyond the immediate environment. There is no reason to suppose that the coherency of the social system as a whole will mean that there will be no conflicts of interest, difficulties in seeing the least cost strategy and so on.

The rural areas of north Vietnam are inhabited by people who have good reasons for valuing collective organization rather highly. They have occupied a region of population saturation for many centuries, and furthermore, have lived with a 'planned economy' since the late 1950s (Vickerman 1986). From a comparative perspective, therefore, north Vietnam provides an extremely interesting environment for examination of how the particular context of agricultural collectivization based upon the Soviet model may result in quite different outcomes. In Vietnam, the operation of the familiar Soviet model of agricultural producer co-operative had some striking peculiarities. Perhaps the most intriguing was the independence from higher levels of local interests within the co-operatives, where, as distinct from the Soviet case, co-operative managers seem almost always to have been local people. Co-operatives retained considerable autonomy, and the basic 'top-down' hierarchical model did not apply.

This outcome was bound up with, and largely resulted, from the systematic series of interactions between, on the one hand, household-based activities and, on the other, those within the collective sphere whose existence was prescribed and supported by party propaganda. These are in many ways familiar from other collectivized areas. But what is most interesting is the way in which relative local autonomy was frequently great enough to determine the content of co-operatives themselves. Often, a co-operative became an empty 'shell', with collective power concentrated at the level of the production brigades (Fforde, 1989, Chapter 3). Negotiations between brigade leaders and co-operators in such co-operatives largely determined the balance between various ways of organizing economic activity.

Since there could be bargaining about the actual operational content of any given co-operative, it follows that the formal system of property rights laid down in official statutes (Fforde, 1984) was not necessarily realizable. The real system of property rights was therefore the result of the social processes involved in determining the actual content of the co-operative, and the activities of other groups and agents, in any given commune. As such, it was something related to, but quite different from, the formal legal system presented by the national State apparatus. It is therefore quite proper to ask the questions given above regarding the nature of property rights, and these then allow one to move some way towards understanding precisely what was meant by the 'private'–'collective' dichotomy in north Vietnamese agriculture. Here space considerations, and a desire to discuss also the implications of the 'output contract' system (see below) preclude a lengthy discussion.

Agents

Here it is possible to identify various agents involved in working out the holding and enforcement of property rights.

Of overwhelming importance was the centre of the party–State apparatus itself, which, through its legal and propagandistic statements, defined the detailed formal system (which was obviously not immutable) that laid down the economic rights of specified agents within the formal system. The statute (Fforde, 1984) is a particularly clear example; note also the use of 'model' co-operatives and their role in the attempted implementation of the so-called 'New Management System' in the mid-1970s (Fforde, 1982; 1989). This placed pressure upon peripheral members of the apparatus for conformity with norms established in this way. This in turn was met by pressure from local interests. But the central party–State apparatus was not closely or directly involved in enforcing property rights in specific instances, which were typically dealt with locally.

This brings us to questions of terminology at the micro-level. What is meant by 'locally'? So far as can be told, local interests usually meant those within a particular 'commune', the traditional administrative rural unit that had always had important corporate functions. By the mid-1970s, co-operatives had been amalgamated so that they were almost always either at commune level, or just below it at 'village' level.

For the sake of illustration, a commune might have 5,000 inhabitants and possibly 300–400 hectares of rice land. It could have two or three villages divided in turn into perhaps a dozen 'hamlets', which usually formed the basis for the mono-cultural rice production brigades responsible for collective production prior to 1979–80. The traditional commune had had important corporate functions, for instance in the regulation of 'private' and 'communal' land. North Vietnamese historians and ethnologists have, with to my mind considerable insight, suggested that from the point of view of the traditional commune, the 'private' land was subject to local – collective – control, whereas the 'communal' land was seen as to a greater extent under the influence of the dynastic state. (See Fforde, 1983: 104, quoting Bui Huy Lo and Nguyen Huu Nghinh 1978: 44; also Nguyen Dong Chi 1964: 50–51.) For a number of reasons, such as the amalgamation of communes into larger units since the Revolution, contemporary 'villages' (*thon* or *lang*) are often old communes, and this level is often of great importance to local sentiments.

Within this group of people, the co-operative(s) could play different roles. Various groups identified with various socio-economic organs, but the basic stand-off was between the management committee of the cooperative, the brigade leaders, and the mass of the co-operators. Each could acquire and dispose of resources in rather different ways.

115

Rights of access and use

In principle, the management committee of a co-operative under the pre-'output contract' (i.e. unreformed) system had extensive rights determining access to and use of economic resources. It could place supply-duties upon the co-operators, not only in terms of labour, but also to obtain other inputs, such as manure, piglets, adult pigs, a share of petty-production returns through taxation of small-scale producers etc. It could take resources from production brigades – land, fixed capital (drying yards and warehouses, draught animals) and require them to surrender all control over the distribution of output produced within them. All this placed a successful committee in an overwhelmingly powerful position, and so it inspired strong opposition on the part of other interests within the collectivity – neither brigades nor co-operators would, without hesitation, respect the obligations imposed upon them. As a result, the formally, i.e. statutorily (Fforde, 1984: 326), approved 'private-plot' area frequently exceeded the norm of 5 per cent of the co-operative's land, while powerful brigades in effect turned the co-operative into a neutralised 'protective inter-mediary' between them and superior agencies that might wish to act contrary to their interest.

Rights of acquisition and disposal

These were strongly influenced by technology and State policy. The co-operatives were, in quite orthodox terms, viewed as the conduit for the extraction of the agricultural surplus, and the State sought to use them for that purpose. Consistently with the coercive implications of 'aggravated shortage', rewards offered were almost always lower than those available elsewhere. Equally conventionally, co-operators were formally entitled to dispose freely of output from their 'private plots', which meant that they had access to markets and barter for output so long as they could show that it was the result of their own labour. This was not hard to do, since they could and did grow rice on their five-per cent-land as well as collectively. Pig-rearing, however, was probably the main source of cash. Since, however, there was very little that could not be produced in all parts of the collectivity, it was hard for the authorities to control unplanned trade once these concessions had been made in the statute. There was therefore scope for complicated inter-actions involving the diversion of resources between sectors in order to exploit such opportunities. For instance, collectively produced rice could be distributed to co-operators with the intention that it be used to capture high 'free market' values.

Interactions between different property relations

Here the role of the 'collectivity' becomes most interesting, for it allows some, albeit rather limited, understanding of the forces acting to reproduce the system as a whole. Recalling that co-operatives were the tax-unit suggests the rather invidious position in which management committees found themselves. They had to find some way of using their formal property rights, which were usually under pressure from brigade cadres and co-operators, to meet delivery targets imposed on them from above. It is reasonable to assume that some part at least of the tax burden was seen as worth avoiding.

Here the committee could attach conditions to the granting of concessions to such pressures in order to allow it to meet its own obligations to higher levels. For example, excess five-per-cent land could be made conditional upon meeting the centrally-imposed target of starting up a collective pigherd. This technique, relying upon the deliberate violation of formal property rights, is very interesting.

The erosion of formal property rights by such processes should perhaps therefore be viewed as essential to the reproduction of the system as a whole, and therefore part of its basic structure.

Local cadres needed to violate the system in order to get things done, and, when this becomes very widespread, it results in such extensive modification of the original collective farm model that something quite different has been created. Systematic illegality is required in order to balance the various interests involved in a sustainable manner, and in so doing helps to determine the real pattern of property rights. In caricature – co-operators get more five-per-cent land, brigade leaders still have their position as bosses of the local collective units required by the party centre, and the committee has something to give to higher levels.

The long-term sustainability of such a system depends on a variety of factors. One, of course, is the willingness of the national leadership to tolerate such goings-on. Another is the stability of the environment faced by collectivities, especially the relative value of participation in different sorts of allocative relations. For instance, a sharp rise in barter opportunities may increase co-operator pressure for greater concessions. Trade across the Sino-Vietnamese border in 1987 was said to be largely barter. Perhaps more importantly, the development issue itself may force people to reconsider the underlying rationale of the system, prompting pressure for reform. One of the main and widely-accepted judgements upon the pre-'output contract' system of co-operative management was its economic inefficiency (Fforde 1989). Cadres who attempted to operate it found continual problems in securing respect for formal property rights, and under prevailing conditions factor productivities –

land yields, output per man, return upon capital – as well as input–output ratios for many current inputs – all tended to be higher in activities based more closely upon non-coercive methods of resource aquisition and disposal, such as certain parts of the formally collective economy as well as much 'own-account' co-operator activity.

More pointedly, if rising population appears to be eroding the subsistence margin, there will be reduced co-operator tolerance for non-working cadres and the economic inefficiency created by unwieldy collectives. Such factors help explain both the crisis nature of the circumstances surrounding the introduction of reforms in 1979–80, and the form they eventually took.

Changes in the early 1980s – the 'output contract' system

In 1979–80 the system of agricultural collectives went through major changes, and by the end of 1980 official policy had radically revised its earlier insistence upon strong centralized co-operative managements in favour of a decentralized system that gave out collective land to groups of co-operators. Pressures for 'decollectivization' do not seem to have been strong enough to result in an abandonment of the system of co-operatives altogether. Certain elements of the 'output contract' system enabled co-operatives to retain income sources that could be used to finance the welfare services that were highly valued by the peasantry.

A notable area of co-operative activity where conflicts did not occur was the use of collective resources to supply seed for improved rice varieties (Fforde 1989, Chapter 10.3). As in the case of local welfare services, when collective behaviour also had an economic rationale, there is no reason to suppose that rational people will support a full-scale return to household-based activity when and if they have the choice. If some collective functions are valued sufficiently highly then there will be pressure for them to be retained. It is worth pointing out that the welfare services are both real and valuable. Consultancy carried out in two delta provinces of the Swedish International Development Agency in 1987 showed beyond reasonable doubt that income support for families with many children and poor labour supply was of great importance; it is also worth noting that the population had, to all intents and purposes, a universal system of at least eight years of schooling. This was run at commune level (see Fforde and Liljestrom 1987).

It was argued above that the balance between sub-systems within the co-operative was influenced by the collectivity's external environment in two main ways: the balance of incentives provided by different ways of acquiring and disposing of resources, and the prescribed norms of the top political leadership. In the late 1970s both of these were to change radically. This happened well before the formal introduction of 'output contracting' in the winter of 1980–1. Between the Sixth Plenum of the Central Committee of the Vietnamese Communist party in August 1979 and the promulgation of Central Directive 100 in January 1981 (Party Secretariat, 1981) there were a number of complicated and naturally largely spontaneous changes in the northern delta areas which effectively pushed for a re-definition of co-operative management norms. At the same time, there were also an important series of conflicts over the way in which rural collectivities should acquire and dispose of resources, which in the event saw the central authorities return to a conservative position after a termporary period of support for freer disposal of mobilized agrarian surplus. But, for many reasons, the degree of coercion within State procurement channels also declined, so that there was a greater respect for material incentives throughout the area. The picture is further complicated by processes of spontaneous decentralization occurring in State industry, which both responded to and supported free-market orientated peasant marketing strategies.

By 1980, reported annual per capita staples output in the northern delta region (for administrative definition see Table 5.1) was down to below 250 kg of paddy equivalent – about equal to 13.5 kg of milled rice per month. There had been a fall of around 10 per cent since national reunification in 1975–6. For almost anybody concerned with the development of the northern economy these were extremely disturbing figures. During the early 1960s, monthly domestic supplies per head had been around 16 kg for the whole of the area covered by the old Democratic Republic of (North) Vietnam. The fall in this indicator to below 13 kg in 1968–9 had been a major factor in precipitating both large-scale Soviet food aid and an open debate about co-operative management methods associated with so-called 'family contracts' (*khoan ho*). These were condemned as simply disbanding the co-operatives by giving the land back to co-operators, despite their apparent success in terms of output in the province where they had been tried – Vinh Phu, in the north of the Red River Delta (Fforde and Paine, 1987: 69, 107, 120).

By the end of 1980, official policy towards co-operative reform had become formalized in what had become known as the 'output contract' (*khoan san pham*) system. This system saw the co-operative allocate the previously collectively farmed land to its members, usually on the basis of the population and/or labour resources of each family. Distribution of the output from this land was governed by a contract signed between the co-operative and the family. This contract had various elements. The so-called contracted amount was divided into two – the co-operative's and the 'output given back to the co-operator'. The contracted amount was typically based upon the average yield over the previous few years, when reported harvests had been poor because the weather had been bad and resource diversion from the collective particularly severe. It was therefore quite easy to fulfil. The category of 'output given back to the co-operator' was meant to be calculated by using the existing system of work norms – so many points for ploughing, transplanting and so on. For example: if the co-operative was going to plough and harrow the contracted field, then this would require so many hours of work, calculated according to the area of land, its ease of ploughing etc. This would then be paid for at the rate of so many points according to the co-operative's system of labour categories (for instance, ploughing might get twelve points a 'labour-day' compared with six points for watching over a grazing buffalo). This sum would then be part of the 'contract', and would be paid to the co-operative by the co-operator. If, however, the co-operator decided that he or she could do the ploughing better themselves, then they would retain this portion of the output.

This system meant that the collective had a basis for retaining the system of distribution of output according to points based upon technical norms. This had important implications. The co-operators in principle retained all output in excess of the contracted amount, thus having a strong stimulus to increase input levels. This was added to their other income in kind, whether it be rice grown on their five-per-cent land, rice 'given back to the co-operators', or earnings elsewhere in the co-operative, and they could treat it in the same way as these other categories.

Contract levels were fixed initially for a number of years. The system allowed co-operatives to retain some control over a local tax base in kind, which allowed them to use rice to help families in need, and to support teachers and other welfare services. It also gave them resources to finance economic activities such as running new seed beds, buying and keeping breeding stock such as boars and entirely non-agricultural activities such as small-scale industry. The other side of the coin, of course, was that there was less rice available for free trade in the local economy. This inhibited the development of small-scale non-agricultural production in sectors that would have had to rely upon the market for rice supplies.

From the point of view of its wider socio-economic implications, however, the reform had three important aspects:

1. Its effect upon the direction of central political pressure for certain internal organizational norms within co-operatives.
2. Its effect upon patterns of State procurement and the extent to which the State has been able to move towards a more voluntary basis of its purchases, and the corollary, its toleration for the free market.
3. Its effect upon patterns of accumulation within rural areas, and the diversification of resources out of staples production into other crops, livestock and/or non-agricultural activities.

Official discussion focused largely upon the first of these three issues. However, until around the time of the Sixth Party Congress of December 1986 the authorities continued to seek directly to control the mobilized staples surplus. There was, however, a public stress on the need to place greater reliance upon material incentives.

The period 1980–6 can be seen as one during which the economy moved increasingly out of control as Marxist-Leninist conservatives in charge of central economic organs tried in vain to defend the central planning system with a series of tactical concessions. Failure to confront macro-economic issues required them to grant massive wage and price concessions which resulted in extremely rapid inflation. Only after the Sixth Congress and the departure of most of the old leaders did realistic reform come back on to the agenda. In the meantime, however, pressure upon peasants to sell cheaply to the State reflected the practical need to compete with the free market in order to push down food prices for urban consumers. This was not sucessful, and city dwellers were forced increasingly on to the free market. By 1982, the proportion of state employees' expenditure on food supplied by the State had fallen to below 25 per cent, compared with around 60 per cent in the second half of the 1970s (Tong cuc Thong ke, 1983: 90, also Fforde, 1988a, Table 12.4). Throughout, however, the co-operatives remained the officially accepted locus of rural accumulation.

In its initial formulation, the 'output contract' system was seen by the conservatives who remained in power as above all a way of strengthening the system of agricultural co-operatives. This was, it was believed, threatened by the weakening in central political commitment to the old managerial system marked by the Sixth Plenum of August 1979 combined with the rapid escalation of co-operator interest in free market opportunities associated with the general movement of the national economy in 1979–80 (Fforde, 1989, Chapter 12). At this time the top leadership was also deeply concerned by the aftermath of the Chinese invasion of early 1979, and it is worth recalling the important role played by the rural areas in providing the disciplined and committed troops that the Vietnamese People's Army had relied upon to reunite the country. However, after an initial period of support for a major shift in policy towards support for the free market (e.g., Nguyen Lam, 1980), the traditional hostility towards petty-commodity production re-affirmed the need to assert the State's right to be the sole purchaser of staples. This was so, although Decree 25-NQ/TU of the Politburo (as quoted in BBC – SWB, 23–04–80) had asserted in early 1980: 'With regard to the management of the grain market, it is necessary to ensure that peasants can freely use or sell the grain that they have left after they have met their obligations to the State.'

By June, however, a second resolution, Decree 26-NQ/TW, superseded this and announced the need to increase state management of domestic trade. This second decree, discussed in the party daily *Nhan Dan* of 24 March 1982, raised agricultural purchase prices and stressed the use of two-way contracts in procurement. It therefore admitted the importance of material incentives.

The sense of policy's 'push' against forces moving the co-operatives in what was seen as the wrong direction comes through strongly from the available literature. Thus the Ministry of Agriculture's Circular Letter No. 05 (1981) clearly details the pattern and justification of re-control, as does the Ministry's report to the early 1981 conference on the whole issue of 'output contracts' (Le Thanh Nghi, 1981). Party Decree 100, issued in January 1981, followed a number of articles (e.g. Huu Hanh, 1980; Nguyen Huy, 1980) in defining the reforms solely in terms of the internal organization of co-operatives.

When viewed in this way the reform was extremely simple. It was based upon the existing norm-governed Tayloristic 'links' of the production process, used for calculating labour remuneration in the collective brigades. By dividing up the production process into discrete tasks which could all be measured and identified, this had provided brigade leaders and co-operative managers with a concrete means for allocating labour and rewards to workers. Now, however, certain of these links were to be the responsibility of contracted co-operators: caring for and lifting seedlings, transplanting seedlings, caring for the growing rice and harvesting. The brigades were to sign contracts with the co-operators on behalf of the co-operative, and surplus output for the State was to be delivered through the co-operative as before. Most surplus output, it was intended, should be delivered to official procurement agencies. The contracts were called 'output contracts' in order to mark the fact that they were closely bound up with linking the co-operative's procurement duties to the co-operators' output, part – or most – of which was contracted to be delivered to the co-operative. Instead of political pressure to rely upon the cumbersome and inefficient brigades, co-operators were now under pressure to permit the co-operative to retain control over production and output disposal. (For a pragmatic guide to how this was to be done see Central Agricultural Management Committee, 1985.)

This overall policy stance lasted until the mid-1980s. An informed editorial in the party theoretical journal *Communist Studies* (1985, No. 5) argued that while the 'output contract' system should be given credit for agricultural recovery (but see below), it needed to be improved. The Sixth Plenum in 1985 therefore stressed a number of points:

1. Co-operative planning was defined as the legally binding two-way contract between the district and the co-operative: deliveries from the co-operative were in return for supplies of production

inputs (no mention was made of consumer goods).

2. Reform of the internal management of co-operatives, with a preservation of the existing brigade and team structure.
3. Expansion of economic activities of the State at the district level, with trade relations made more economic and efficient by moving away from subsidies.

State policy therefore sought to maintain the co-operative as both a focal point for political pressure in the rural areas and as the main channel for surplus mobilization. But this position did not go unchallenged (e.g., Dao Xuan Sam, 1982).

One of the most interesting pointers to the reality of the 'output contract' system was the criticism of 'white contracts'. These are best seen as empty contracts, whereby the co-operative management simply gave out land to co-operators, without providing any collective inputs. There was a clear sense underlying many official commentaries that the system needed continual strengthening (e.g., Propaganda, 1984). Clearly, talk of 'white' contracts, like the earlier talk of 'ghost' co-operatives, referred to situations where the formal property system was not widely respected, for there was institutionalized disobedience of its norms.

Aggregate results and the gathering subsistence crisis in the northern deltas

The performance of northern agriculture over the past decade cannot be isolated from the more general difficulties facing the Vietnamese, and especially the north Vietnamese, economy. Broadly speaking, these can be characterized by the cumulative effects of over-investment and over-urbanization in areas without the capacity to support such activities, aggravated in the north by the inefficiencies of the neo-Stalinist development model adopted by the DRV (Fforde and Paine, 1987; for south Vietnam, see Dacy, 1986). From 1980–1 economic policy sought to defend the central planning system with a series of tactical concessions, of which the 'output contracts' were part. But resource demands from the State sector were too high, and rapid inflation soon developed as the State was forced to print money in order to defend its own. At the same time it became more and more difficult to prevent dynamic growth processes arising in the richer regions, especially the south. To a certain extent, this has isolated the poorer areas from the rest of the economy, aggravating the gathering subsistence crisis.

In terms of the initial reported staples output gains *for the entire country*, the immediate results of the new policy appear to have been extremely good. Both measured total agricultural output and staples production rose faster than total population (see Table 5.1). But this hides important regional differences, above all between over-populated areas and the relatively land-rich south. The output response in the long-collectivized provinces of the north appears to have been substantial. Provincial output data is not available for some years and this prevents a direct assesment of the output gain in the north during 1979–80. Despite this, the increase of 1981 over 1980 was quite substantial. Furthermore, the available data does suggest that almost all of the output gain in 1979–80 came in the Mekong delta of south Vietnam, where the collectivization drive had been temporarily halted. In 1981, the year when the new policy was formally introduced into the agricultural co-operatives dominant in the north and centre, there was a sharp jump in output in those regions. This came on top of the recovery in the south in the previous year, and created substantial breathing space for the Vietnamese economy as a whole.

After 1981, however, the north saw a general stagnation in output, so that, on a *per capita* basis, the steady long-term deterioration continued (see Table 5.2). By 1984, top leaders were deeply concerned:

> Just recently the food deficient area (*dien thieu doi*) was very large, as were the numbers of people going hungry. But the numbers who were short of food, and the numbers going hungry were not clear. If the area concerned was indeed as large as local reports maintained, then that would have been a great cause for concern. But if the food deficit area was large, but the hungry area was small, then that would have been another matter altogether. One can ask and ask but it is impossible to get a clear idea of the real position. But one really needs to get a good analysis of the concrete situation, although one does not know how to do so. When I heard about the situation, I myself was very worried, for *since the August Revolution* our country has never faced a comparable food shortage in the north. There are many reasons for this situation. (Le Duc Tho, 1984: 462. Emphasis added.)

The importance of Le Duc Tho's remark about the August Revolution should not be underestimated. The August Revolution of 1945 occurred in the aftermath of the terrible 1944–5 famine which killed at least one million Vietnamese, and played a major part in generating popular support for the Viet Minh and Ho Chi Minh's Declaration of Independence in September of the same year (Woodside, 1976: 232–3).

Le Duc Tho's analysis of the situation is basically conservative in not acknowledging the adverse effects upon the northern economy of the central planning system and the implicit confrontation with the free market. He points out that the output contract system had only produced a once-for-all jump in output. He goes on to argue, however, that further gains depended upon technological changes, and so, implicitly, that further reforms and greater reliance upon decentralization could not be a source of sustained advance. According to this view, the basic constraints upon such improvements to the agrarian base were:

1. the fact that agriculture was still essentially small-scale; and
2. the fact that industry still met many difficulties.

Furthermore, a major part of the output gains in recent years were simply the result of good weather. Bad weather would put things back severely, and it was therefore quite wrong to go around saying that the country was self-sufficient 'n food when they had only just reached 300 kg of staples per head and year (Le Duc Tho, 1984: 464). In an interesting aside, he asserted that the Soviet Union is not such a good model in any case. After nearly seventy years of Soviet power they had only just got to 200 million tonnes of staples, despite the fact that agriculture was heavily supplied with industrial inputs. 'And now in the Soviet Union agriculture is not only the centre of the economic problem but also a political problem as well' (Le Duc Tho, 1984: 464). Le Duc Tho is no slavish supporter of the Soviet Union. However, his data for Vietnam include rice and non-rice staple, while the figure of 200 million tonnes of the Soviet Union excludes non-grain staples such as potatoes. He also neglects to mention that staples output per head in the Soviet Union was, in 1985, at nearly 700 kg and therefore more than double the Vietnamese level.

This is a position that seems to marry a defence of the rationing inherent in the Soviet central planning system with the functions of collectives in coping with risk and uncertainty. It is not easy to argue against this position in the absence of further research. However, it is worth pointing out that there is little scope within it for the changes in the pattern of accumulation needed to generate some form of sustainable growth within the northern deltas. The old view, which was that accumulation should only occur within 'progressive' sectors – in agriculture, the state farms and co-operatives – meant that local 'entrepreneurs' had, in practice, to come from the ranks of local co-operative cadres, and to rely upon the co-operatives. Profits would have to be shared out, and would have to contribute to local taxes. It also supported local conservative cadres in their hostility to accumulation in areas outside the collective, which would both threaten their own personal power base and those amongst the peasantry who saw such social differentiation as a threat to collective welfare.

These are very real problems. By the mid-1980s, north Vietnamese agriculture was so poor that its integration into the world economy would pose considerable difficulties. Rice production could not be expected to generate the economic surpluses that would finance additional inputs without subsidies. The vagaries of the weather added to the factors pushing for popular support for collective institutions that provided welfare services and income support. This made it harder to generate incentives for those who might be in a position to create rural employment outside agriculture. Life was still hard and risky.

It followed that extremely flexible policies and strategies were needed, and, for people living so near to subsistence and under such risky and uncertain conditions, these methods would have to respect and utilize collective forms. Since the best hope for the generation of non-agricultural employment was in small-scale industry, this suggested the need to exploit any strong entrepreneurial skills within co-operatives, which were by no means necessarily present. Large profits made by individual households could be seen as disruptive to the collectivity, and also a threat to cadres' position. More support from the State was needed to encourage and underwrite flexible methods, and this in turn required a relaxation of political pressure for conformity with certain norms, and a heightened respect for material incentives. The latter could, however, be seen in various measures adopted after the Sixth Party Congress, such as the dismantling of inter-regional trade controls early in 1987. At the time of writing, however, the outlook, while far better than at almost any time since the end of the war, is far from clear.

Editor's postscript

Recent statistics of the Council of Mutual Economic Assistance, to which Vietnam as a member state supplies a slowly increasing amount of data, so far have not formed the basis for an optimistic outlook. They show livestock numbers and meat production of private owners increasing, but total output of rice per head of the population declined from 265 kilograms in 1985 to 262 kg in 1986, and 242 kg by 1987, while that of other grains remained at an insignificant 13 kg.[7]

Appendix (Statistical Tables)

Table 5.1: Output per head, paddy equivalent per annum (kg)

Area	1976	Year 1981	1984
Hanoi	247.5	128.2	128.6
Haiphong	174.6	194.6	194.0
Vinh Phu	209.5	205.7	203.5
Ha Bac	289.1	307.2	248.4
Quang Ninh	125.0	117.8	138.1
Ha Son Binh	183.0	263.4	263.9
Hai Hung	352.3	392.3	316.4
Thai Binh	363.0	352.8	330.3
Ha Nam Ninh	321.5	275.8	289.8
Thanh Hoa	230.0	261.4	270.9
Nghe Tinh	220.1	217.9	232.8
Northern deltas[a]	255.0	251.3	243.2
- as % of total	–	91.7	–
Vietnam	274.8	274.1	304.0

Note: (a) This is defined as: Hanoi, Haiphong, Vinh Phu, Ha Bac, Quang Ninh, Ha Son Binh, Hai Hung, Thai Binh, Ha Nam Ninh, Thanh Hoa and Nghe Tinh.
Source: *Tong cuc Thong ke* (Statistical Office), Statistical Materials, various tables and years.

Table 5.2 Percentage changes in output per head, paddy equivalent per annum (kg)

Area	1981/76	1982/81	Year 1984/82	1984/81	1984/76
Hanoi	−48.2	12.5	−10.8	0.3	−48.1
Haiphong	11.4	12.9	11.7	−0.3	11.1
Vinh Phu	−1.8	−22.5	27.6	−1.1	−2.9
Ha Bac	6.2	0.6	−19.6	−19.1	−14.1
Quang Ninh	−5.8	11.1	5.6	17.2	10.5
Ha Son Binh	−43.9	−4.8	5.3	0.2	44.2
Hai Hung	11.3	−0.3	−19.1	−19.4	−10.2
Thai Binh	−2.8	4.2	−10.2	−6.4	−9.0
Ha Nam Ninh	−14.2	15.0	−8.6	5.1	−9.9
Thanh Hoa	13.6	3.0	0.6	3.6	17.8
Nghe Tinh	−1.0	1.1	5.7	6.8	5.8
Northern deltas[a]	−1.5	3.0	−6.0	−3.2	−4.7
Vietnam	−0.3	9.9	0.9	10.9	10.6

Note: (a) Defined as in Table 5.1.
Source: As for Table 5.1.

Table 5.3 Some general data on Vietnamese agriculture (1985)

Total population of the Socialist Republic (million)	59.87
Value of gross agricultural output (billion 1982 dong)	91.04
Of which – cultivation	70.14
livestock	21.12
(Does not sum to total in original)	
Staples production:	
Total (million tonnes unmilled paddy equivalent)	18.20
Area (million hectares)	6.83
Rice (million tonnes paddy)	15.87
Area (million hectares)	5.70
Staples supplied to the state	
(million tonnes unmilled paddy equivalent)	3.91
Livestock (million)	
Numbers – Buffalo	2.59
Oxen	2.60
Pigs (over two months)	11.81
Pork production (ex-stye live weight, million tonnes)	0.56
Pork supplied to the state	
(live weight, million tonnes)	0.26
Labour of working age (million)	16.19
Number of agricultural co-operatives	16,334
Number of state farms	414
Tractors, all types physical units (of 15.2 nominal kW/h on average[a])	45,029

Note: (a) Derived from *Statisticheskii ezhegodnik strau-chlenov Soveta Ekonomicheskoi Vzalmopomoshchi, 1987*: 213.
Source: *Tong cuc Thong ke* (Statistical Office), Statistical Yearbook, 1987; Tables 1, 23, 27, 68.

Notes

1. Adam Fforde is Economic Consultant and Research Associate, Queen Elizabeth House, Oxford University. One-time ESRC Post-Doctoral Research Fellow, Department of Economics, Birkbeck College, London University. This chapter is partly based upon work funded by the Economic and Social Research Council, and is also part of the programme of research into the role of the private sector in collectivized agriculture instigated by Prof. K.-E. Wädekin and sponsored by the Stiftung Volkswagenwerk.
2. All those who have done work on modern Vietnam, and are therefore familiar with the practical difficulties involved, will know that this is not intended as a criticism of our limited results.

3. Here the term coercion is of course used relatively, since relations *within* the agent voluntarily supplying resources may be far from voluntary. Intra-familial relations are an example that springs immediately to mind.

4. The stress in this assertion should be read as resting upon the term 'established'. There appears much in the literature on 'market failure' that can usefully be applied to decision making under conditions of aggravated shortage, and this can be seen in the econometric analysis of disequilibrium in developed centrally planned economies. I am not aware of a comparable literature on 'plan failure', but see Ellman (1979) for some extremely interesting comments, drawing again upon the strands of bounded rationality and uncertainty that inform discussions of 'market failure'. Ellman's attempts to develop these ideas do not appear to be common in the literature.

5. By 'risk' is here understood a potential cost whose probability could be gauged by those who face it; by 'uncertainty', I understand a potential cost (or benefit) to which no probability may be attached – people simply do not know. Scott (1976) is the classic work on the effects of risk upon rural social organization in non-collectivized rice-growing areas. The identification of risk and uncertainty, and the implications for collective behaviour, as one important consequence of 'aggravated short-age' is, although to my knowledge new, merely an extension of Scott's thinking to modern north Vietnamese conditions. See also Loasby (1976), Lavoie (1985) and the discussion in Ellman (1979: 65–79).

6. Thus, with regard to the psychology of collectivised peasants in Soviet Asia, it has been nicely observed that the State has replaced Nature as the basic source of uncertainty in people's lives (Humphrey 1983).

7. The editor's source is *Statisticheskii ezhegodnik stran-chlenov Soveta Ekonomicheskoi Vzaimoposhchi 1988*, Moscow 1988: 196 (recalculated index), 233–41 and 244, from which the following data are also taken:

	1985	1986	1987
Index of total agricultural production	100	104	104
of which: livestock production	100	107.5	116
Sown area, thsd hectares	7840	7846	7686
Livestock numbers, thsd per end of year			
horned cattle, incl. buffaloes and oxen	5188	5441	5732
of which in individual ownership			
(per cent)	51.8	62.9	65.9
pigs (over two months)	11808	11796	12051
of which in individual ownership			
(per cent)	96.9	97.7	97.4
Total meat output (thsd tonnes,			
live weight)	749	833	1016

References

Note: Quotations in the text from various Vietnamese legal documents are

from the Official Gazette *Cong Bao*, published in Hanoi. Until 1986 the
Statistical Office produced a yearly collection entitled *So lieu thong ke*
(Statistical Materials); in 1986 this was not published and in 1987 the
Office produced a larger volume entitled *Nien giam thong ke* (Statistical
Yearbook).

Central Agricultural Management Committee (1985) *Hoi dap ve Khoan san
pham trong hop tac xa* (Questions and answers on output contracts in
agriculture), Hanoi.
Dacy, D.C. (1986) *Foreign Aid, War, and Economic Development: South
Vietnam, 1955–1975*, Cambridge.
Dao Xuan Sam (1982) 'Van de loi ich kinh te trong thuc tien quan ly kinh
te hien nay' ('The problem of economic interests in economic
management at present'), *Economic Research*, 128.
Ellman, M. (1979) *Socialist Planning*, Cambridge.
Fforde, A.J. (1982) *Problems of Agricultural Development in North
Vietnam*, Doctoral dissertation, Cambridge University.
Fforde, A.J. (1983) *The Historical Background to Agricultural
Collectivization in North Vietnam: the Changing Role of 'Corporate'
Economic Power*, Birkbeck College, Dept. of Economics, Discussion
Paper 148.
Fforde, A.J. (1984) 'Law and socialist agricultural development in Vietnam
– the Statute for Agricultural Producer Cooperatives', *Review of
Socialist Law*, 10.
Fforde, A.J. (1988) 'Specific aspects of the collectivization of wet-rice
cultivation: Vietnamese experience', in J.C. Brada and K.-E. Wädekin
(eds) *Socialist Agriculture in Transition*, Boulder and London.
Fforde, A.J. (1989) *The Agrarian Question in North Vietnam, 1974–79: A
Study of Cooperator Resistance to State Policy*, New York.
Fforde, A.J., Liljestrom, R., Ohlsson, B. (1988) *Forestry Workers in
Vietnam – A Study on the Living and Working Conditions*, SIDA,
Stockholm.
Fforde, A.J., Paine, H.S. (1987) *The Limits of National Liberation*,
London.
Humphrey, C. (1983) *Karl Marx Collective – Economy, Society and
Religion in a Siberian Collective Farm*, Cambridge.
Huu Hanh (1980) 'Khoan lua (rice contracts)', *Communist Studies*, 12.
Kornai, (1980), *The Economics of Shortage*, 2 vols, Amsterdam.
Lavoie, D. (1985) *Rivalry and Central Planning: the Socialist Calculation
Debate Reconsidered*, Cambridge.
Le Thanh Nghi (1981) *Cai tien Cong tac khoan mo rong khoan san pham
de thuc day san xuat cung co hop tac xa nong nghiep (Reform contract
work and expand output contracts to stimulate production and reinforce
agricultural cooperatives)*, Hanoi.
Le Duc Tho (1984) 'Mot so van de kinh te, xa hoi truoc mat' (Some
immediate socio-economic problems), in *Xay dung dang trong cach
mang xa hoi chu nghia o Viet nam (Party construction during the
Vietnamese socialist revolution)*, Hanoi.

Loasby, B.J. (1976) *Choice, Complexity and Ignorance: An Enquiry into Economic Theory and the Practice of Decision-making*, Cambridge.

Ministry of Agriculture (1981) *Huong dan viec thuc hien cai tien cong tac khoan trong cac hop tac xa san xuat nong nghiep* (Guiding the realization of contract work in agricultural co-operatives), Circular Letter, Hanoi.

Nguyen Dong Chi (1964) 'Mot so diem quan he den che do gia dinh cua nguoi Viet Nam thoi co dai' ('A number of points relating to the Vietnamese family system in ancient times'), *Nghien cuu lich su*, 109.

Nguyen Huy (1980) 'Ve hinh thuc khoan trong lua trong hop tac xa trong lua' ('On forms of contracting in rice cultivating co-operatives'), *Nghien cuu kinh te*, 118.

Nguyen Lam (1980) 'May van de ve tu tuong chinh sach kinh te hien nay' ('Some problems in economic thinking at the present time'), *Communist Studies*, 3.

Nguyen Duc Nghinh and Bui Huy Lo (1978) 'May van de nghien cuu ruong dat cong trong cac lang xa nguoi Viet dau the ky 19' ('Some problems of research into communal land in the Vietnamese villages of the nineteenth century'), *Tap chi dan toc hoc*, 2.

Nove, A. (1977) *The Soviet Economic System*, London.

Party Secretariat (1981) *Cai tien cong tax khoan, mo rong khoan san pham den nhom nguoi lao dong va nguoi lao dong trong hop tac xa nong nghiep* (*Reform of contract work, expansion of output contracts with groups of workers and individual workers in agricultural cooperatives*), Hanoi.

Propaganda (1984) 'Ve tinh hinh khoan "trang" trong nong nghiep va cach khac phuc' ('On "white" contracts in agriculture and ways of getting rid of them'), *Tuyen truyen (Propaganda)*, 5.

Scott, J.C. (1976) *The Moral Economy of the Peasant*, Yale University Press.

Tong cuc thong ke (Statistical Office), various years, *So Lieu thong ke (Statistical Materials)*, Hanoi.

Tong cuc Thong ke (Statistical Office) (1987) *Nien giam thong ke* (Statistical Yearbook), Hanoi.

Vickerman, A. (1986) *The Fate of the Peasantry: Premature 'Transition to Socialism' in the Democratic Republic of Vietnam* (Monograph Series, No. 28, Yale University SEA Studies), Yale Centre for International and Area Studies.

Wädekin, K.-E. (1973) *The Private Sector in Soviet Agriculture*, Berkeley, Los Angeles, London.

Wädekin, K.-E. (1982) *Agrarian Policies in Communist Europe*, Dordrecht.

Werner, Jayne (1984) 'Socialist development – the political economy of agrarian reform in Vietnam', *Bulletin of Concerned Asian Scholars*, 2.

White, C.P. (1982) 'Family and class in the theory and practice of Marxism – the case of Vietnam', *IDS Bulletin*, 4.

Woodside, A.B. (1976) *Community and Revolution in Modern Vietnam*, Boston.